COOKING WITH
Bon Appétit

COOKING WITH
Bon Appétit

American Regional Favorites

THE KNAPP PRESS
Publishers
Los Angeles

Copyright © 1985 by Knapp Communications Corporation

Published by The Knapp Press
5900 Wilshire Boulevard, Los Angeles, California 90036

Library of Congress Cataloging in Publication Data

Main entry under title:

American regional favorites.

  (Cooking with Bon appétit)
  Includes index.
   1. Cookery, American. I. Bon appétit. II. Series.
TX715.A5085 1985   641.5973   85-14647
ISBN 0-89535-169-2

On the cover (clockwise from top): *Yankee Scallop and Clam Chowder; tossed green salad
with Winter Vinaigrette; Plymouth Prime Rib; Pear and Turnip Puree; Lemon-Chive
Butter; Hubbard Squash Pie in Walnut Crust; Maple Syrup Mousse; Herbed Buttermilk
Biscuits*

Printed and bound in the United States of America

10   9   8   7   6   5   4   3   2

❦ Contents

❦ *Foreword*

A marriage of immigrant culinary traditions and native ingredients, American cooking is as splendid in its scope and variety as any of the great world cuisines. This collection of over 200 *Bon Appétit* recipes celebrates our rich legacy of American foods, from New England cranberries and maple syrup to the tortillas and chilies of the sunny Southwest.

Given our diverse landscapes, climates and ethnic groups it is no wonder that the nation's cooking has evolved along distinctly regional lines. Pennsylvania Germans, Southern blacks, French and Spanish settlers in New Orleans and Mexican-Americans in the Southwest—among many others—have all shaped the cuisines of their respective areas. And these days the West Coast, in particular, is coming increasingly under the sway of Oriental cooking.

Because it is formed of such numerous and disparate influences, "American cuisine" can be difficult to define. It comprises countless dishes from around the globe which have been adapted to locally available products—as well as true New World inventions like gumbo, whose distinctive ingredient, filé powder, was introduced to Louisiana Creole cooks by the Choctaw Indians.

Compared to European and Asian cuisines that have been refined over many centuries, our gastronomic heritage is brief and still in active development. As James Beard put it in 1972, "We are barely beginning to sift down into a cuisine of our own"—but we are finding the process a tremendous pleasure.

1 ❦ Appetizers

A great appetizer adds a note of festivity to any meal. It may be served with predinner cocktails or at the table; it may be a simple dip for chips or crudités, or an elegant presentation such as Shad Roe with Asparagus (page 11). In any case, it always seems to lift the menu from the routine and to make the meal a special occasion.

This collection of appetizers and first courses encompasses a wide spectrum of dishes with one thing in common: All are uniquely American. The flavors of the Southwest enliven such zesty openers as Savory Cheese and Chile Churros (page 6), Cornmeal Pancakes with Green Chile Salsa (page 3), and Creamy Chile con Queso Dip (page 11). The West Coast offers Artichokes with Green Goddess Dressing (page 2), California Crudités with Herb Cream (page 2), and Dungeness Crab with Red Pepper Mayonnaise (page 8). From the South come unusual oyster specialties and Angel Biscuits with Herb Butter (page 5), topped with paper-thin rounds of country ham.

Many of these recipes can be made ahead and served without fuss, giving the cook a chance to finish any last-minute preparations for the rest of the meal.

Vegetable Appetizers

Artichokes with Green Goddess Dressing

Green Goddess dressing is a San Francisco invention. It was first concocted at the Palace Hotel in the 1920s to honor George Arliss, who was starring on Geary Street in a play entitled The Green Goddess.

2 servings

4 quarts water
2 artichokes
1 lemon, halved

¼ cup fresh lemon juice
3 tablespoons olive oil
2 teaspoons salt
2 bay leaves
10 whole black peppercorns
    Pinch of cayenne pepper

4 teaspoons chopped anchovies
1 tablespoon minced fresh parsley

2 teaspoons minced green onion
2 teaspoons minced fresh tarragon
    or pinch of dried, crumbled
2 teaspoons tarragon wine vinegar
2 teaspoons whipping cream
1 teaspoon snipped fresh chives
1 teaspoon fresh lemon juice
½ cup mayonnaise, preferably
    homemade

Bring water to boil in large pot. Meanwhile, cut 1 inch off top of each artichoke with scissors. Snip sharp tip off each leaf. Remove small leaves at bases. Break off stems. Rub bases of artichokes with cut lemon.

Add ¼ cup lemon juice, oil, salt, bay leaves, peppercorns and cayenne to water. Add artichokes and return to boil. Cover and cook until bases are tender when pierced with skewer, 40 to 50 minutes. Drain well. Cool slightly.

Mix anchovies, parsley, onion, tarragon, vinegar, cream, chives and 1 teaspoon lemon juice in small bowl. Whisk in mayonnaise. Cover dressing and refrigerate until ready to use.

To serve, set artichokes on plates. Pass dressing separately.

California Crudités with Herb Cream

10 servings

Herb Cream (makes 1½ cups)
1 egg, room temperature
1½ tablespoons fresh lemon juice
2 teaspoons Dijon mustard
½ teaspoon salt
2 dashes hot pepper sauce
    Freshly ground pepper
1 cup vegetable oil
⅓ cup well-chilled whipping cream
½ cup minced fresh basil or
    3 tablespoons dried, crumbled

¼ cup chopped fresh parsley
2 tablespoons snipped fresh chives
1 tablespoon minced fresh thyme
    or 1 teaspoon dried, crumbled

Fresh fennel sticks, carrots, cherry tomatoes, Belgian endive spears, snow peas and radish roses

For cream: Combine egg, lemon juice, mustard, salt, hot pepper sauce and pepper in processor and mix well. With machine running, add oil through feed tube in thin steady stream and mix until thickened. Add cream, basil, parsley, chives and thyme and mix 15 seconds using on/off turns. Taste and adjust seasonings. Turn herb cream into small serving dish. Cover and refrigerate at least 2 hours or overnight. Let stand at room temperature for 30 minutes before serving.

Arrange vegetables on large platter and set cream in center for dipping.

Cornmeal Pancakes with Green Chili Salsa

For best results, have all of the ingredients at room temperature.

Makes about 32 2-inch pancakes

8 ounces mild green chilies*

Green Chili Salsa
2 tablespoons vegetable oil
⅓ cup minced green onion (white part only)
2 pounds tomatillos
Salt and freshly ground pepper
¼ cup sour cream or crème fraîche

Cornmeal Pancakes
¼ cup (½ stick) butter
¾ cup all purpose flour
¼ cup yellow cornmeal

½ teaspoon baking powder
3 ounces cream cheese
¾ cup milk
3 egg yolks
½ cup corn kernels (1 medium ear)
3 egg whites
½ teaspoon salt
Pinch of cream of tartar

2 tablespoons clarified butter (or more) or 1 tablespoon butter and 1 tablespoon oil
Cilantro leaves (optional garnish)

Preheat broiler. Arrange chilies on pan. Roast 6 inches from heat source, turning until blackened on all sides, about 6 minutes. Transfer to plastic bag and seal tightly. Let stand 10 minutes to steam. Peel charred skin from chilies and discard. Remove cores, seeds and veins. Rinse chilies if necessary and pat dry; mince finely, reserving 1 chili for pancake batter.

For salsa: Heat oil in heavy large saucepan over medium heat. Add green onion and stir until transparent, about 3 minutes. Add minced chilies and stir to coat with oil. Remove from heat. Puree tomatillos in processor or blender. Press

---

 ### How to Roast and Peel Fresh Chilies

Chilies are often roasted to enhance their flavor and facilitate peeling. Three methods are given here. All work well, so experiment and use the one you find most convenient.

Oven method: Preheat broiler. Cut small vertical slit in chili to prevent bursting. Arrange on baking sheet. Broil 4 inches from heat until blistered and charred on all sides, about 6 minutes, turning every few minutes.

Electric stove method: Set heatproof rack on burner. Cut small vertical slit in chili to prevent bursting. Arrange chilies in center of rack so that all will come in contact with heat source. Turn heat to medium-high and roast chilies until blistered and charred on all sides, about 4 minutes, turning often.

Gas stove method: Cut small vertical slit in chili to prevent bursting. Spear with fork (or use tongs). Turn each chili over high flame until blistered and thoroughly charred on all sides.

To peel, immediately transfer chilies to plastic bag and seal. Freeze 10 minutes. (*Chilies can be frozen six months. Thaw before continuing.*) Skin, seed and stem chilies. Devein if desired (veins and seeds provide the heat).

Tips

- When handling chilies, wear gloves or generously oil hands as chili oils can cause burning or skin irritation. Always wash hands with soap and water after handling chilies.
- Avoid looking down feed tube of food processor or blender while grinding as fumes can be irritating.

pulp through very fine strainer into chili mixture, discarding seeds. Place over medium-high heat and bring to boil. Let boil until mixture is thickened and reduced to about 1½ cups. Season with salt and pepper. (*Can be prepared ahead to this point, cooled, covered and refrigerated. Rewarm before proceeding.*) Reduce heat to medium-low. Stir in sour cream; do not boil or mixture will curdle.

For pancakes: Melt butter in small saucepan. Set aside to cool. Sift flour with cornmeal and baking powder. Beat cream cheese, milk and egg yolks in large bowl of electric mixer until well blended. Stir in cornmeal mixture, corn, reserved minced chili and melted butter. Beat egg whites in large bowl until foamy. Add salt and cream of tartar and continue beating until whites are stiff but not dry. Gently stir ¼ of whites into batter, then fold batter into remaining whites.

Preheat oven to 175°F. Melt clarified butter on griddle or in heavy skillet over medium heat. Ladle 2-inch pancakes onto griddle. Cook until bottom is medium brown and unbroken air bubbles form on top, about 2 to 3 minutes. Turn and brown second side. Repeat with remaining batter, buttering griddle as necessary. As pancakes are finished, arrange in single layer on ungreased baking sheet in oven. Spoon salsa in center of 4 heated serving plates and surround with pancakes. Garnish with cilantro leaves if desired. Serve immediately.

*Any type of chili can be used as long as proportion is adjusted for desired spiciness.

Roasted Pumpkin Seeds

These can be served plain or mixed with butter and sugar or salt and garlic.

Pumpkin seeds, rinsed and patted dry

Spread seeds in single layer on paper towel-lined baking sheet. Dry at room temperature 8 hours or overnight.

Preheat oven to 375°F. Spread seeds in single layer on unlined baking sheet. Bake until golden brown, stirring occasionally, about 12 minutes. Serve hot or at room temperature.

Noel's Pumpkin Curls

8 servings

1 1-pound wedge of pumpkin

Peanut oil (for deep frying)

1 1 × ¾-inch chunk fresh ginger, finely grated

Cut pumpkin into 2- to 3-inch-wide wedges. Discard stringy interior. Starting at inside, peel off paper-thin strips of pulp down full length of wedges, using vegetable peeler. (*Can be prepared 1 day ahead. Cover and refrigerate.*)

Preheat oven to 200°F. Line baking sheets with paper towels. Heat oil in large saucepan to 375°F. Fry ginger until golden brown, about 1 minute. Transfer to prepared sheets using slotted spoon. Keep warm in oven. Fry pumpkin in batches (do not crowd) until brown and crisp, about 1 minute, skimming oil between batches. Transfer to prepared sheets, using slotted spoon or tongs, and keep warm in oven. Alternate layers of pumpkin and fried grated ginger in napkin-lined basket. Serve immediately.

🍎 *Appetizer Pastries*

Angel Biscuits with Herb Butter

These dainty Southern appetizers are difficult to resist. The extra unfilled biscuits can be frozen, but they also make a good accompaniment to the main course. If any of the greens are not available, use watercress.

Makes about 6 dozen

½ envelope dry yeast
¼ cup warm water (105°F to 115°F)
2½ cups sifted all purpose flour
1½ tablespoons sugar
1½ teaspoons baking powder
½ teaspoon baking soda
¼ teaspoon salt
6 tablespoons solid vegetable shortening
1 cup buttermilk

3 tablespoons unsalted butter, melted
⅓ cup minced turnip greens

8 ounces thinly sliced country ham or Black Forest ham
Herb Butter*

Grease medium bowl. Sprinkle yeast over warm water in small cup; stir to dissolve. Resift flour with sugar, baking powder, baking soda and salt 3 times. Place in processor. Cut in shortening using on/off turns until mixture resembles coarse meal. With machine running, pour yeast and buttermilk through feed tube and process until dough just comes together. Knead on lightly floured surface until smooth, about 30 seconds. Place in greased bowl, turning to coat entire surface. Cover and refrigerate at least 1 hour. (*Can be prepared 3 days ahead.*)

Preheat oven to 400°F. Grease baking sheets. Roll dough out on lightly floured surface to thickness of ½ inch. Cut into 1-inch rounds using cookie cutter. Brush tops with butter and sprinkle with greens. Arrange on prepared sheets, spacing ½ inch apart. Bake until golden, about 12 minutes.

Cut ham into 36 rounds using 1-inch cookie cutter. Split 36 biscuits and spread with herb butter. Sandwich ham round between each. (*Can be prepared 2 hours ahead. Wrap in foil and rewarm in 350°F oven 10 minutes.*) Serve warm. Pass remaining biscuits separately with herb butter.

*Herb Butter

Makes about 1 cup

1 cup (2 sticks) unsalted butter, room temperature
1 tablespoon minced fresh parsley
1 tablespoon minced watercress

1 tablespoon minced turnip greens
1 tablespoon minced dandelion greens
1 tablespoon snipped fresh chives

Blend butter in processor until smooth. Mix in remaining ingredients. Transfer to small bowl. (*Can be prepared 2 days ahead and refrigerated. Bring to room temperature before using.*)

Cream Biscuits with Ham and Sweet and Rough Mustard

Makes about 2 dozen

Biscuits
4²/₃ cups pastry flour
2 tablespoons baking powder
2 tablespoons sugar
1 teaspoon salt
3 cups whipping cream
¹/₂ cup (1 stick) butter, melted
¹/₄ cup minced fresh parsley

Mustard
¹/₂ cup coarse-grained mustard
¹/₂ cup Dijon mustard
¹/₂ cup honey
¹/₄ cup finely chopped mango chutney

Baked ham slices

For biscuits: Preheat oven to 375°F. Sift flour, baking powder, sugar and salt into large bowl. Add cream and stir gently with fork until dough comes together. Turn dough out onto lightly floured surface and roll into ¹/₂-inch-thick rectangle. Brush some of butter across half of dough. Sprinkle parsley over butter. Fold dough in half horizontally. Cut dough into rounds using 2-inch cutter. Arrange rounds on baking sheets. Brush tops with remaining butter. Bake until puffed and golden, about 15 minutes.

For mustard: Blend all ingredients.

To serve, split biscuits in half horizontally. Spread bottom halves with mustard. Top each with ham slice. Cover with top halves.

Savory Cheese and Chili Churros

A variation of a classic sweet fritter.

Makes 12 to 14

1 cup plus 2 tablespoons water
3 tablespoons butter, chopped
Pinch of salt
³/₄ cup all purpose flour
¹/₄ cup white cornmeal
2 eggs

3 jalapeño peppers, stemmed, seeded and minced
2 tablespoons freshly grated Monterey Jack cheese

Peanut oil (for deep frying)

Combine water, butter and salt in heavy medium saucepan and cook over medium heat until butter melts. Remove from heat. Immediately mix in flour and cornmeal with wooden spoon. Set over medium-high heat and stir until mixture pulls away from sides of pan to form ball and begins to form film on bottom, 1 to 2 minutes. Transfer to processor. Cool for 5 minutes. Blend in eggs one at a time. Add peppers and cheese and mix until smooth.

Heat oil in deep fryer or heavy deep skillet to 375°F. Spoon dough into pastry bag fitted with No. 5 star tip. Pipe 10-inch strips into oil in batches without crowding. Fry until golden brown, about 3 minutes per side. Drain on paper towels and serve.

Cheddar Chili Cheesecake

12 servings

1¹/₂ tablespoons butter (for pan)
¹/₄ cup fine breadcrumbs, lightly toasted
¹/₄ cup finely grated sharp cheddar cheese

6 ounces thinly sliced ham
1¹/₂ pounds cream cheese, room temperature
12 ounces sharp cheddar cheese, grated

1 cup cottage cheese
³/₄ cup chopped green onions
4 eggs
3 tablespoons seeded and finely chopped jalapeño pepper
2 tablespoons milk
1 garlic clove, halved

Preheat oven to 325°F. Butter 9-inch springform pan. Mix breadcrumbs and ¼ cup cheddar. Sprinkle mixture into pan, turning to coat. Refrigerate.

Dice about half of ham; reserve remaining slices. Mix diced ham with remaining ingredients in blender or processor until smooth. Pour slightly more than half of filling into prepared pan. Top with reserved ham slices in even layer. Cover with remaining filling. Set pan on baking sheet. Bake 1¼ hours. Turn oven off and cool cheesecake about 1 hour with door ajar. Transfer cheesecake to rack. Remove sides of pan. Cool cheesecake to room temperature before serving.

Cajun Meat and Oyster Pies

Makes 24

Pastry
2½ cups unbleached all purpose flour
1 teaspoon sugar
1 teaspoon salt
½ cup (1 stick) frozen butter, cut into 1-inch pieces
1 egg, beaten to blend
½ cup well-chilled milk

Meat and Oyster Filling
½ cup bacon drippings
1 pound lean ground pork
½ cup all purpose flour
6 green onions, chopped
1 medium onion, chopped
1½ cups chicken stock
½ cup drained oysters, liquor reserved
Salt and freshly ground pepper
Hot pepper sauce

1 egg beaten with 2 tablespoons milk (glaze)

For pastry: Mix flour, sugar and salt in processor using 3 to 4 on/off turns. Blend in butter and egg with on/off turns until mixture resembles coarse meal. With machine running, pour milk through feed tube and blend until dough just starts to hold together; do not form ball. Turn out onto work surface and shape into disc. Wrap in plastic and refrigerate 1 hour.

For filling: Melt bacon drippings in heavy large skillet over medium heat. Add pork and brown, crumbling with fork. Remove with slotted spoon. Reduce heat to low. Add flour and stir with wooden spoon until hazelnut color, about 25 minutes. Add onions and cook until slightly wilted. Blend in stock, oyster liquor and seasonings and cook until thick, about 15 minutes. Add oysters and cook just until firm. Adjust seasonings. Set aside.

Preheat oven to 375°F. Grease baking sheet. Roll dough out on lightly floured surface into circle ¼ inch thick. Using 3-inch cutter, cut out dough circles. Gather scraps. Refrigerate 30 minutes. Reroll and cut additional circles. Place 2 tablespoons filling in center of each circle. Brush edges with egg glaze. Fold dough over filling, sealing edges with fork tines. Transfer to prepared baking sheet. Refrigerate 30 minutes. Brush both sides of pies with egg glaze. Bake 15 minutes. Turn each over and continue baking until golden brown, about 10 more minutes. Serve immediately.

Seafood Appetizers

Dungeness Crab with Red Pepper Mayonnaise

10 servings

Red Pepper Mayonnaise
(makes 2¼ cups)
- 1 large red bell pepper

- 1 tablespoon chopped shallot
- 2 egg yolks, room temperature
- 1½ tablespoons fresh lemon juice
- 2 teaspoons Dijon mustard
- ½ teaspoon salt or to taste

- ¼ teaspoon freshly ground white pepper
- 3 generous pinches of cayenne pepper
- 1⅓ cups safflower oil

- 2 large or 3 medium-size cooked* fresh Dungeness crabs (about 5 pounds total), cracked

For mayonnaise: Preheat broiler. Roast pepper 6 inches from heat source, turning until blackened on all sides. Transfer to plastic bag and steam 10 minutes. Peel pepper, discarding veins and seeds. Rinse, if necessary, and pat dry with paper towels. Chop coarsely.

Transfer to processor. Add shallot and puree until smooth, scraping down sides of bowl twice. Add yolks, lemon juice, mustard, salt, white pepper and cayenne and mix until smooth, stopping machine and scraping down sides of bowl twice. With machine running, pour oil through feed tube in slow steady stream. Taste and adjust seasoning. Transfer mayonnaise to small serving dish. Cover and refrigerate until ready to use. (*Can be prepared up to 1 day ahead.*)

To serve, fill deep large platter with layer of crushed ice. Set bowl of mayonnaise in center. Surround with crab.

*To cook live crab, drop crab head first into large amount of rapidly boiling salted water over high heat. Return water to boil. Cook crab until very tip of leg pulls off easily without meat, about 15 minutes. Let cool before cracking into serving pieces.

Chesapeake Oysters and Smithfield Ham en Brochette

10 servings

- 30 fresh oysters, shucked
- 30 4 × 4-inch paper-thin slices

Smithfield, Westphalian or Black Forest ham (about 7½ ounces)

Preheat indoor grill or prepare outdoor barbecue. Wrap each oyster tightly in 1 slice of ham and secure each with bamboo skewer. Grill until charred, about 5 minutes, turning once. Serve hot.

Oysters Bayou Teche with Sage Cream

8 servings

- ¼ cup bacon drippings
- ½ cup chopped green onions
- 6 tablespoons all purpose flour
- ½ cup half and half
- 1 cup sour cream
- ¼ cup dry white wine
- 2 tablespoons minced fresh Italian parsley
- 1 tablespoon minced fresh sage or 1 teaspoon dried, crumbled

- 2 teaspoons Worcestershire sauce
- 1 teaspoon salt
- ½ teaspoon cayenne pepper
- ¼ teaspoon freshly ground pepper
  Hot pepper sauce
- 3 dozen oysters, shucked (reserve bottom shells and ½ cup liquor)

- ¾ cup fresh breadcrumbs tossed with ¼ cup freshly grated Parmesan cheese

Melt bacon drippings in heavy large skillet over medium heat. Add green onions and sauté 2 minutes. Remove from heat. Slowly stir in flour with wooden spoon to make smooth roux. Return skillet to medium heat. Stir in half and half to make smooth thick paste. Reduce heat to low. Add next 9 ingredients. Blend in ½ cup oyster liquor and stir 5 minutes; do not boil or sauce will curdle. Taste and adjust seasoning.

Preheat oven to 400°F. Pat oysters dry. Wash and dry 36 bottom shells; arrange on baking sheets. Place 1 oyster in each. Top with sauce. Sprinkle with breadcrumb mixture. Bake until light golden crust forms, about 15 minutes. Serve oysters immediately.

Baked Oregano Oysters

12 servings

Herbed Mushroom Sauce
½ cup (1 stick) butter
1 cup minced green onions
¾ cup minced fresh parsley
1 garlic clove, minced
½ cup all purpose flour
2 cups half and half
4 egg yolks, room temperature, beaten to blend
⅔ cup finely chopped fresh mushrooms
2 tablespoons chopped fresh oregano or 1½ to 2 teaspoons dried, crumbled

1 tablespoon anise liqueur
⅛ to ¼ teaspoon cayenne pepper
1 teaspoon salt
½ teaspoon freshly ground pepper

2 to 3 dozen fresh unshucked oysters

Rock salt
8 ounces cooked bacon, finely crumbled

For sauce: Melt butter in heavy large saucepan over low heat. Add onions and ¼ cup parsley with garlic. Cover and cook until onion is limp, about 10 minutes. Gradually stir in flour. Whisk 3 minutes; do not brown. Gradually whisk in half and half, then yolks. Blend in mushrooms, oregano, liqueur and cayenne. Continue cooking until thick, stirring frequently. Add salt and pepper. Pour sauce into medium bowl and let cool. Refrigerate 2 to 3 hours.

To shuck oysters, hold oyster knife in writing hand; hold oyster tightly in opposite hand with rounded side up and hinged part of shell in palm. Insert end of knife between shells near hinge and twist to pry shells open partially. Work knife blade around shells to sever hinge. Pry top shell off with hands and discard. Work knife around oyster to release from shell. Drain oysters well. Transfer oysters to airtight container and refrigerate until ready to use. Scrub bottom oyster shells and set aside. (*Oysters can be shucked several hours ahead and stored on ice.*)

Preheat oven to 500°F. Line 2 to 3 ovenproof trays or platters with ½-inch layer of rock salt. Arrange oyster shells in salt. Place 1 oyster in each shell. Spread 1 tablespoon sauce over each oyster. Sprinkle tops with bacon and remaining parsley. Bake until sauce browns lightly, about 15 to 18 minutes. Cool oysters slightly before serving.

Oysters on the Half Shell with Three Sauces

The ideal way to serve oysters to a crowd is oyster-bar style. Arrange the necessary equipment for shucking the oysters—two or more oyster knives, heavy-duty waterproof canvas gloves and a plastic bag for the empty shells—along with the sauces, napkins, toothpicks and crackers on a table so guests can serve themselves.

12 servings

72 **fresh unshucked oysters, rinsed**

Cold Mustard Sauce*

Pickled Pepper Sauce**
Black Pepper Sauce***

Place oysters in large tub or barrel with water and large chunks of ice until ready to serve (oysters will spoil quickly if not kept very cold).

To shuck, hold oyster knife in writing hand; hold oyster tightly in opposite hand with rounded side up and hinged part of shell in palm. Insert end of knife between shells near hinge and twist to pry shells open partially. Work knife blade around shells to sever hinge. Pry top shell off with hands and discard. Work knife around oyster to release from shell. Sprinkle or spoon sauce onto oyster and "drink" oyster and liquor; or use toothpick to dip oyster into one of the sauces.

---

*Cold Mustard Sauce

Makes about 1½ cups

1 **cup mayonnaise**
¼ **cup whipping cream**
2 **tablespoons chopped green onion**
1 **tablespoon chopped capers**
1 **tablespoon chopped fresh parsley**
2 **teaspoons coarse-grained French mustard**

2 **teaspoons fresh tarragon or**
½ **teaspoon dried, crumbled**
2 **teaspoons fresh lemon juice**
1 **teaspoon Worcestershire sauce**
¼ **teaspoon freshly ground pepper**
Dash of hot pepper sauce

Whisk all ingredients in small bowl. Cover; refrigerate until ready to serve.

**Pickled Pepper Sauce

Makes about 2 cups

2 **cups fresh red or green chilies**
2 **garlic cloves, sliced**

2 to 3 **fresh dill sprigs**
2 **cups white vinegar**

Combine chilies, garlic and dill in 1-quart jar. Bring vinegar to boil. Pour vinegar over chilies. Cover jar tightly. Let stand in cool place at least 2 days to mellow. To serve, strain sauce into small bowl; discard garlic and dill.

***Black Pepper Sauce

Makes about 1½ cups

1 **cup catsup**
¼ **cup water**
2 **tablespoons freshly ground pepper**

1 **tablespoon cider vinegar**
1 **tablespoon fresh lemon juice**
1 **teaspoon cayenne pepper**
½ **teaspoon salt**

Mix all ingredients in small bowl. Cover; refrigerate until ready to serve.

Shad Roe with Asparagus

10 servings

5 pairs shad roe
10 teaspoons butter
10 teaspoons dry white wine
10 teaspoons fresh lemon juice
2½ teaspoons chopped fresh tarragon
Salt and freshly ground pepper

½ cup (1 stick) butter, melted
Juice of 1 medium lemon

30 asparagus spears (about
1½ pounds), stalks snapped
at natural breaking point

Vegetable oil (for frying)
10 lemon wedges

Separate each pair of roe into halves. Center 1 half on right side of 12 × 12-inch square of waxed paper. Dot with 1 teaspoon butter; drizzle with 1 teaspoon wine and 1 teaspoon lemon juice. Sprinkle with ¼ teaspoon tarragon. Season with salt and pepper. Fold paper over and roll up edges to seal. Repeat with remaining halves. (*Can be prepared up to 2 hours ahead to this point.*)

Blend melted butter and lemon juice. Cook asparagus in large pot of boiling salted water until crisp-tender.

Meanwhile, pour oil into large skillet to depth of ¼ inch. Heat oil over medium heat. Preheat oven to lowest temperature. Add roe packages to oil in batches and cook until paper is browned, about 4 minutes on each side. Keep roe warm in packages in oven. Drain asparagus and pat dry. Unwrap roe and transfer to individual heated plates. Arrange 3 asparagus stalks on side of each roe. Drizzle asparagus with lemon butter. Garnish with lemon wedges and serve.

 *Dips*

Creamy Chili con Queso Dip

This is a perfect dip for tortilla chips, but it can also double as a side dish with Tex-Mex menus. Hotter chilies may be used.

8 servings

8 ounces sharp cheddar cheese, grated
1 12-ounce can chopped green chilies, drained
3 cups sour cream

8 ounces mild cheddar cheese, grated
8 ounces Monterey Jack cheese, grated

Preheat oven to 375°F. Layer ⅓ of sharp cheddar, chilies, sour cream, mild cheddar and Monterey Jack in 8 × 8-inch baking dish. Repeat layering twice. Bake until cheese is melted and center is set, about 30 minutes. Serve hot.

Hot Mushroom Dip

Makes 2½ to 3 cups

4 slices bacon
8 ounces fresh mushrooms, sliced
1 medium onion, finely chopped
1 garlic clove, minced
2 tablespoons all purpose flour
¼ teaspoon salt
⅛ teaspoon freshly ground pepper

8 ounces cream cheese, cut into small pieces
2 teaspoons Worcestershire sauce
2 teaspoons soy sauce
½ cup sour cream
Crackers and breadsticks

Fry bacon in large skillet over medium heat until crisp. Drain, reserving 2 tablespoons drippings in skillet. Crumble bacon and set aside. Add mushrooms, onion and garlic to reserved drippings and cook over medium heat until tender and most of mushroom liquid has evaporated, about 6 to 8 minutes. Mix in flour, salt and pepper. Add cream cheese, Worcestershire and soy sauce. Reduce heat to low and stir until cheese is melted. Remove from heat. Stir in sour cream and bacon. Serve warm with assorted crackers and breadsticks.

Hot Crab Dip

8 servings

1 8-ounce package cream cheese, room temperature
1 6-ounce can crabmeat, drained
2 tablespoons minced green onion

1 tablespoon milk
1 teaspoon prepared horseradish
$\frac{1}{8}$ teaspoon freshly ground pepper
Raw vegetables for dipping

Preheat oven to 350°F. Oil 1-quart soufflé dish. Mix all ingredients except raw vegetables in medium bowl. Turn into prepared dish. Bake until bubbly, about 30 minutes. Serve crab dip hot with vegetables.

Shrimp and Cheese Dip

Serve with crackers or cocktail rye.

Makes 4 generous cups

1 pound cream cheese, room temperature
$\frac{2}{3}$ cup cottage cheese (5 ounces)
8 ounces frozen tiny shrimp, thawed and drained well
3 tablespoons minced roasted and peeled red bell pepper

1 teaspoon minced fresh garlic
1 teaspoon Dijon mustard
Hungarian paprika, salt and coarsely ground pepper to taste

Combine cream cheese and cottage cheese in large bowl and beat until light and fluffy. Fold in all remaining ingredients. Transfer dip to crock or serving bowl. Cover and chill until ready to serve.

2 ❦ Soups

America's regional cuisines boast a magnificent array of soups, from silken-textured bisques to ribsticking Yankee chowders. The signature ingredients of any area always turn up in its soups; this collection, for example, features New England oysters and clams, Maryland crab and Minnesota wild rice, among many others.

All the soups in this chapter make perfect first courses. Such easy-but-elegant offerings as Bisque of Butternut Squash with Apple (page 17), Cream of Celery Root and Bourbon Soup (page 18), and Pecan Cream Soup La Hacienda (page 21) can begin even the most formal dinner party in grand style. Others are ideal for family suppers and casual entertaining. For example, Southern Style Crab Soup (page 17), Kidney Bean Chowder (page 19), and Minnesota Wild Rice Soup (page 22) are a feast in themselves if accompanied by crusty bread or biscuits and a salad.

You will find yourself returning again and again to this assortment of distinctive American soups. There is something here for every taste, every occasion, every cook.

 *Seafood Soups*

Corn Cream with Scallops and Ham

Perfect for beginning an elegant dinner. Accompany with a chilled fruity white wine such as Riesling or Chenin Blanc.

4 to 6 servings

3 tablespoons unsalted butter
8 large shallots, thinly sliced
½ teaspoon sugar
5 cups fresh corn kernels (about 7 ears) or two 10-ounce packages frozen
2½ cups Basic Stock*
2 cups milk
1 cup whipping cream
⅛ teaspoon freshly ground white pepper
Pinch of freshly grated nutmeg

6 ounces Westphalian or cooked Smithfield ham, cut into ¼-inch cubes
Salt
8 ounces sea scallops, quartered
½ cup corn kernels

Melt butter in heavy 4-quart saucepan over low heat. Add shallots. Cover and cook until tender, stirring occasionally, about 10 minutes. Stir in ½ teaspoon sugar. Increase heat to medium and cook uncovered until sugar just turns golden, stirring frequently, about 5 minutes. Mix in corn, stock, milk, cream, pepper and nutmeg. Bring to boil. Immediately remove from heat. Puree mixture through fine blade of food mill. (*Can be prepared 1 day ahead and refrigerated.*)

Bring soup to simmer in heavy medium saucepan. Add ham and simmer 30 seconds. Add salt. Add scallops and ½ cup corn. Immediately remove from heat. Adjust seasoning and serve.

*Basic Stock

This ample recipe should supply you with enough stock for months of good soup making. Let the stock simmer the entire 14 hours for fullest flavor.

Makes 6 quarts

8 pounds chicken necks and backs or wings, or whole stewing chicken, cut into small pieces
5 pounds cooked or uncooked meat and poultry bones (beef, veal, chicken, turkey, duck or goose), trimmed and cut into small pieces
2 pounds veal breast, trimmed, boned (bones reserved) and meat cut into ½-inch pieces

6 large onions, coarsely chopped
4 large carrots, coarsely chopped
3 large celery stalks with leaves, chopped
3 parsley sprigs
6 garlic cloves
6 whole cloves
4 large bay leaves
1 tablespoon dried basil, crumbled

Place first 3 ingredients in 16-quart stockpot. Add enough cold water to cover by 3 inches. Slowly bring to boil, skimming surface occasionally. Reduce heat so water simmers gently, cover partially and cook 5 hours.

Add all remaining ingredients to stockpot. Pour in enough water to cover by 2 inches. Bring to simmer. Cover partially and cook 8 to 9 hours.

Strain stock through fine sieve, pressing to extract as much liquid as possible. Pour into clean pot. Boil, uncovered, until stock is reduced to 6 quarts. Cool, then refrigerate. (*Can be stored in refrigerator 4 days or frozen up to 4 months.*) Degrease stock before using.

Yankee Scallop and Clam Chowder

Serve with hot biscuits for a satisfying first course.

10 servings

4 ounces salt pork, rind removed, cut into ½-inch dice
2 slices thick-cut smoked bacon, cut into 1-inch squares

2 large leeks, cut crosswise into ½-inch slices (white and 1 inch of light green parts only)
2 small carrots, sliced ¼ inch thick
½ large onion, thinly sliced
1 cup ¼-inch-thick slices tender inner celery stalks
3 cups Rich Fish Stock*
1 large celery root, peeled, trimmed and cut into ¾-inch cubes

3 thyme sprigs, tied
1 small bay leaf

½ cup dry white wine or vermouth
18 clams, rinsed and scrubbed

2 cups whipping cream
½ teaspoon sugar
¼ teaspoon saffron threads, crushed
8 ounces fresh bay scallops or halved sea scallops
Pinch of cayenne pepper
Salt and freshly ground pepper

1½ tablespoons minced fresh parsley

Cook salt pork and bacon in heavy 6-quart saucepan over medium heat until crisp, stirring occasionally. Remove with slotted spoon and drain on paper towels. Do not clean saucepan.

Add leeks, carrots, onion and celery to same saucepan and cook over medium heat until slightly colored, stirring occasionally, about 15 minutes. Add fish stock, celery root, thyme and bay leaf. Reduce heat and simmer gently until celery root is just tender, 10 to 12 minutes; do not overcook.

Meanwhile, pour white wine into steamer. Arrange clams on rack and place in steamer. Cover partially and steam just until clams open; discard any that do not open. Remove clams from shells. Strain steaming liquid through sieve lined with dampened cheesecloth. Add to leek mixture.

Add cream to saucepan and warm through over medium-low heat. Dissolve sugar and saffron in 1 tablespoon chowder. Add scallops and reserved clams to saucepan. Remove from heat. Stir in saffron mixture and cayenne. Season with salt and pepper. Let chowder stand 1 to 2 hours.

Just before serving, reheat chowder; do not boil. Ladle into bowls. Garnish with parsley, salt pork and bacon.

*Rich Fish Stock

Makes about 2 quarts

2½ pounds fish bones and trimmings from nonoily white fish
4 cups water
2 cups dry white wine
2 cups white wine vinegar
2 medium onions, sliced
4 celery stalks, cut into thirds
12 parsley sprigs

6 fresh thyme sprigs or ½ teaspoon dried, crumbled
4 fresh tarragon sprigs or 1 tablespoon dried, crumbled
16 white peppercorns
6 whole cloves
1 teaspoon coarse salt

Combine all ingredients in large nonaluminum pot. Simmer 30 minutes, skimming occasionally. Strain through fine sieve lined with dampened cheesecloth. Cool. (*Can be made 1 day ahead and refrigerated or 1 month ahead and frozen.*)

Clam and Oyster Bisque

This shellfish soup captures the flavors of New England. Serve with freshly baked biscuits.

4 servings

16 cherrystone clams
1 cup dry white wine

½ cup (1 stick) unsalted butter
1 cup chopped leek
(white part only)
½ cup chopped onion
3 medium shallots, chopped

2 teaspoons curry powder
16 oysters, shucked, liquor reserved

3 egg yolks
¾ cup whipping cream
Salt and freshly ground pepper
Minced fresh parsley

Combine clams and wine in heavy medium saucepan. Cover and steam over high heat until clams open. Remove clams from shells. Strain liquid.

Melt butter in heavy large saucepan over medium heat. Add leek, onion, shallots and curry powder and cook until vegetables are soft, stirring occasionally, about 15 minutes. Stir in strained cooking liquid and bring to boil. Add oysters and their liquor.

Transfer mixture to processor. Add clams and chop coarsely using on/off turns. Blend yolks with cream. Return clam mixture to saucepan and place over low heat. Slowly whisk in egg mixture and heat through; do not boil. Season with salt and pepper. Garnish with parsley and serve.

Maryland Crab Soup

Plenty peppery, this soup is filled with snowy chunks of crabmeat.

8 servings

3 tablespoons unsalted butter
2 large yellow onions, coarsely chopped
2 large celery stalks, coarsely chopped
1 large carrot, coarsely chopped
½ large green bell pepper, cored, seeded and coarsely chopped
1 large bay leaf
½ teaspoon dried thyme, crumbled
¼ teaspoon cayenne pepper
¼ teaspoon freshly ground pepper
1 pound beef or veal knuckle bones
3 large new potatoes, peeled and cut into ½-inch dice

1 cup diagonally cut green beans (about ½ inch long)
3½ cups beef broth, preferably homemade
3 cups water

⅓ cup pearl barley

1 1-pound can whole peeled tomatoes, pureed with juice
½ teaspoon salt

1 pound lump crabmeat
¼ cup chopped fresh parsley

Melt butter in heavy large saucepan or Dutch oven over medium heat. Add onions, celery, carrot and bell pepper and stir until lightly browned, about 10 to 12 minutes. Add bay leaf, thyme, cayenne and pepper and stir 2 to 3 minutes. Add bones, potatoes and beans and cook, stirring constantly, 2 to 3 minutes. Blend in broth and 2 cups water. Reduce heat to low, cover and simmer 1 hour.

Add barley and remaining 1 cup water to soup. Cover and simmer 2 hours.

Discard bones. Stir in tomato puree and salt. Let soup cool to room temperature. Cover and refrigerate at least 12 hours. Degrease if necessary.

Discard bay leaf. Stir crab and parsley into soup. Place over low heat and warm slowly, stirring as little as possible to keep crab in large pieces; do not boil or crab will be tough. Season to taste with salt and cayenne pepper. Ladle soup into bowls and serve.

Southern Style Crab Soup

Makes 8 cups

½ cup (1 stick) butter
¼ cup all purpose flour
4 cups milk
2 tablespoons chopped onion
2 teaspoons instant chicken bouillon powder
2 teaspoons minced fresh parsley
1 teaspoon salt

½ teaspoon freshly ground pepper
½ teaspoon freshly grated nutmeg
8 ounces backfin crabmeat
8 ounces fresh asparagus,* trimmed, peeled and cut into 1-inch lengths

Melt butter in heavy large saucepan over medium-low heat. Whisk in flour and cook 3 minutes. Gradually whisk in milk. Add onion, bouillon, parsley, salt, pepper and nutmeg. Increase heat and bring to boil. Reduce heat and simmer until soup begins to thicken, stirring occasionally, about 10 minutes. Add crabmeat and cook until soup is creamy, 10 to 15 minutes. Add asparagus and cook until crisp-tender, 5 to 7 minutes. Adjust seasoning. Serve immediately.

*If unavailable, frozen asparagus can be substituted. Thaw, drain and pat dry before adding to soup.

❦ *Vegetable and Other Soups*

Bisque of Butternut Squash with Apple

6 servings

6 cups rich chicken stock, preferably homemade
1 large butternut squash, peeled and cubed (about 6 cups)
2 medium-size tart green apples, peeled, cored and chopped
1 medium onion, chopped
1½ teaspoons sugar
1 teaspoon salt
Pinch of dried rosemary, crumbled
Freshly ground pepper

2 tablespoons (¼ stick) butter
2 tablespoons all purpose flour
2 tablespoons dry Sherry
2 egg yolks, room temperature
½ cup whipping cream, room temperature

Combine stock, squash, apples, onion, sugar, salt, rosemary and pepper in heavy large saucepan and bring to boil. Reduce heat and simmer until squash is tender, about 1 hour.

Transfer squash mixture to blender and puree until very smooth. Return to saucepan and bring to boil.

Melt butter in another heavy large saucepan over medium-low heat. Whisk in flour and cook 3 minutes. Whisk in squash puree and simmer 5 minutes. Mix in Sherry. Beat yolks and cream in small bowl. Blend in some of hot soup. Whisk mixture back into soup. Rewarm if necessary; do not boil. Serve hot.

Acorn Squash Soup

6 servings

2 pounds acorn squash, halved and seeded

2 tablespoons (¼ stick) butter
2 large leeks (white part only), chopped
5 cups chicken stock, preferably homemade

1 tablespoon tomato paste
1 large thyme sprig or ½ teaspoon dried, crumbled
Freshly ground white pepper

¼ cup whipping cream
Snipped fresh chives

Preheat oven to 350°F. Arrange squash cut side down in roasting pan. Add ½ inch water. Bake until squash begins to soften, about 30 minutes.

Melt butter in heavy large saucepan over medium heat. Add leeks, cover and cook until translucent, stirring occasionally, about 5 minutes. Scoop out squash pulp and add to leeks. Blend in stock, tomato paste, thyme, salt and pepper. Simmer until squash is very soft, about 20 minutes. Cool slightly. Discard fresh thyme (if using).

Puree soup in blender (in batches if necessary) until smooth. Press through fine strainer. (*Can be prepared 1 day ahead and refrigerated.*) Rewarm soup in heavy medium saucepan over medium-low heat. Stir in cream and heat through; do not boil. Ladle soup into bowls. Sprinkle with chives. Serve hot.

Carrot Soup

8 servings

3 tablespoons unsalted butter
2 pounds carrots, chopped
2 large onions, sliced
2 potatoes (about 1 pound), peeled and chopped

1 bay leaf
6 cups (or more) chicken stock

Salt and freshly ground pepper
Minced fresh parsley

Melt butter in Dutch oven or other large saucepan over low heat. Add carrot and onion. Cover with circle of waxed paper and let sweat about 8 minutes. Add potatoes, bay leaf and enough stock to cover vegetables. Cover and simmer until vegetables are tender, about 40 minutes. Discard bay leaf.

Puree soup in batches in processor or blender. Return to saucepan and season with salt and pepper to taste. Place over medium heat and bring to boil, stirring occasionally. Ladle into bowls and garnish with minced parsley.

Additional chicken stock can be added to puree if thinner soup is preferred.

Cream of Celery Root and Bourbon Soup

From the Auberge du Soleil in Rutherford, California, this soup is a superb example of celery root's renewed popularity.

Makes 11 cups

9 tablespoons butter
3 pounds celery root, peeled and cut into 1-inch dice
3 medium baking potatoes, peeled and cut into 1-inch dice
1 medium onion, diced
1 bunch chives (about 10), minced
⅛ teaspoon dried marjoram, crumbled

4 cups rich chicken stock, preferably homemade
5 ounces (½ cup plus 2 tablespoons) bourbon
Salt and freshly ground white pepper

4 cups whipping cream

Melt 6 tablespoons butter in heavy large saucepan over low heat. Add celery root, potatoes, onion, chives and marjoram. Cover and cook until onion is translucent, stirring frequently, about 10 minutes. Blend in stock and bourbon. Season with salt and pepper. Increase heat to medium-high and cook until vegetables are tender, stirring occasionally, about 20 minutes.

Transfer mixture to blender in 4 batches; add 1 cup cream to each batch and blend until smooth. Return to heavy large saucepan. Rewarm soup over low heat. Whisk in remaining 3 tablespoons butter 1 tablespoon at a time, incorporating each piece completely before adding next. Adjust seasoning. Ladle soup into bowls and serve.

White Corn Chowder

If fresh white corn is un-available, canned white corn can be used.

8 servings

2 quarts water
7 ears fresh white corn, husked (pale inside husks reserved)*

¼ cup (½ stick) unsalted butter
1 onion, finely chopped
¼ cup all purpose flour
3 cups whipping cream
¼ teaspoon sugar

¼ teaspoon cayenne pepper
Salt and freshly ground white pepper

Roasted Peppers
1 red bell pepper
1 yellow bell pepper

Cilantro leaves

Bring 2 quarts water to boil in large saucepan. Cook corn cobs and husks 1 minute. Remove cobs and reserve. Reduce heat and simmer husks 30 minutes. Strain liquid. Boil to reduce to 4 cups if necessary. Cut corn from cobs.

Melt butter in heavy 4-quart saucepan over medium-low heat. Add onion and cook until golden brown, stirring occasionally, about 8 minutes. Add flour and stir 3 minutes. Mix in corn cooking liquid. Boil 5 minutes, stirring frequently. Reduce heat and simmer 30 minutes to blend flavors, stirring occasionally. Add cream and simmer until slightly thickened, about 30 minutes. Add sugar, cayenne, salt and white pepper. Cool to room temperature. Refrigerate 4 hours.

For peppers: Char peppers over gas flame or under broiler, turning occasionally, until skin blackens. Wrap in plastic bag and let stand 10 minutes. Peel and seed peppers; rinse if necessary. Cut into thin strips.

Just before serving, bring soup to simmer. Stir in 3¾ cups corn kernels and simmer until hot. Garnish with roasted pepper strips and cilantro.

*If white corn is unavailable, use husks from yellow corn for stock and three 12-ounce cans white corn for kernels. Do not parboil canned white corn.

Kidney Bean Chowder

3 to 4 servings

4 ounces bacon, cut into ½-inch pieces

½ cup chopped onion
½ cup chopped green bell pepper
½ cup chopped celery (including leaves)
1 tablespoon all purpose flour
1 15½-ounce can red kidney beans, undrained

½ cup thinly sliced carrots
2 tablespoons chopped fresh parsley
1 bay leaf
⅛ teaspoon dried thyme, crumbled
2 beef bouillon cubes
2 cups water
Salt and freshly ground pepper

Sauté bacon in 2½-quart saucepan over medium-high heat until crisp. Remove with slotted spoon and set aside. Drain all but 3 tablespoons fat from pan.

Add onion, green pepper and celery to pan and sauté over medium-high heat until softened, about 5 minutes. Remove from heat and stir in flour. Add beans, carrots, parsley, bay leaf, thyme, bouillon cubes and water and blend well. Bring to boil over medium-high heat. Reduce heat, cover and simmer 40 minutes. Season with salt and pepper. Ladle into bowls. Garnish with reserved bacon and serve.

Creole Onion Soup

6 servings

¼ cup smoked ham drippings or bacon drippings
3 tablespoons unsalted butter
1 pound onions, thinly sliced
12 ounces red onions, thinly sliced

¼ cup all purpose flour
7½ ounces smoked ham, trimmed and coarsely chopped (1½ cups)
2 tablespoons fresh lemon juice
1 tablespoon firmly packed light brown sugar
1½ teaspoons Hungarian sweet paprika
½ teaspoon freshly ground pepper

½ teaspoon dried thyme, crumbled
¼ teaspoon cayenne pepper
¼ teaspoon ground allspice
¼ teaspoon ground cloves
¼ teaspoon ground mace
¼ teaspoon hot pepper sauce
5 cups rich beef broth
1 cup dry white wine

2 cups whipping cream
3 tablespoons Cognac
Salt
6 oven-toasted French bread slices
Creole Butter*

Melt drippings and butter in heavy large pot over medium-low heat. Add onions and cook until golden, stirring occasionally, about 30 minutes.

Reduce heat to low. Stir in flour and cook 5 minutes; do not brown. Add ham, lemon juice, sugar, paprika, pepper, thyme, cayenne, allspice, cloves, mace and hot pepper sauce and cook 5 minutes to blend flavors, stirring occasionally. Pour in broth and wine. Increase heat and bring to simmer. Cover partially; simmer 45 minutes.

Puree soup in batches in processor using on/off turns; soup should have slightly grainy texture. Return soup to same pot. Blend in cream and cook over medium-low heat until thick, about 20 minutes. Add Cognac and cook 5 minutes. Adjust seasoning with salt and hot pepper sauce. Spread bread with Creole butter. Ladle soup into bowls. Top with bread and serve.

*Creole Butter

Makes 1 cup

2 medium garlic cloves, halved
½ teaspoon salt
2 teaspoons grated lemon peel
10 tablespoons (1¼ sticks) unsalted butter, room temperature
⅓ cup sliced green onion (white part only)

¼ cup sliced green onion (tender green part only)
2 tablespoons parsley sprigs
Freshly ground white pepper

Mix garlic and salt in processor until paste forms. Blend in lemon peel using on/off turns, scraping down sides of bowl. Add butter, green onion and parsley and mix 60 seconds, scraping down sides of bowl. Blend in white pepper to taste. Transfer to bowl. Refrigerate until ready to use. (*Can be prepared 1 day ahead.*) Bring to room temperature 20 minutes before using.

Pecan Cream Soup La Hacienda

8 to 10 servings

2 tablespoons (¼ stick) butter
1 cup finely chopped celery
1 cup finely chopped leek (white part only)
2¾ cups pecans
⅓ to ½ cup firmly packed light brown sugar (depending on sweetness of tomatoes)
1 ½-inch piece cinnamon stick
2 whole cloves

1 small bay leaf
8 cups chicken stock, preferably homemade
1 cup peeled, seeded and coarsely chopped tomato
1 cup whipping cream
Salt
Pinch of freshly grated nutmeg (optional)
¼ cup toasted pecan halves

Melt butter in Dutch oven over low heat. Add celery and leek and cook, stirring occasionally, until tender, about 10 minutes. Add 2¾ cups pecans, brown sugar, cinnamon stick, cloves and bay leaf and cook 10 minutes, stirring occasionally. Add stock and tomato and blend well. Increase heat to medium and bring to simmer. Let simmer until pecans are tender, about 2 hours. Discard cinnamon stick, cloves and bay leaf. Transfer mixture to blender (do not use processor) in batches and puree until smooth. Return to Dutch oven and bring to boil over high heat. Remove from heat and stir in cream. Season with salt and nutmeg. Ladle soup into heated bowls. Garnish with pecan halves and serve.

Cutlass Potato Soup

8 servings

5 bacon slices
2 tablespoons (¼ stick) butter
3 medium-large boiling potatoes, peeled and chopped
4 medium celery stalks, chopped
1 large carrot, chopped
½ medium onion, chopped

3 cups water
2 teaspoons salt
⅛ teaspoon freshly ground pepper
2 cups milk
2 tablespoons cornstarch dissolved in ½ cup cold water

Fry bacon in heavy large saucepan over medium-high heat until crisp. Remove with slotted spoon; drain on paper towels. Crumble bacon and set aside. Pour off drippings. Melt butter in same pan over medium heat. Add vegetables and cook until slightly softened, stirring occasionally, about 15 minutes. Add bacon, water, salt and pepper. Cover and simmer until vegetables are tender, about 20 minutes. Add milk and heat through. Stir in dissolved cornstarch and cook until soup thickens, about 5 minutes. Serve immediately.

Tomato Dumpling Soup

From the Willow Inn, a restored 1816 farmhouse in Waynesburg, Pennsylvania.

8 servings

1 cup (2 sticks) butter
1 large onion, coarsely chopped
4 16-ounce cans peeled tomatoes, seeded and cut into chunks (liquid reserved)
2 cups (or more) chicken stock
⅓ cup sugar
1 teaspoon cinnamon
1 teaspoon salt
Pinch of freshly ground pepper

1 cup all purpose flour
1 teaspoon baking powder
3 eggs
2 tablespoons vegetable oil
½ medium-size green bell pepper, seeded and coarsely chopped

Melt ½ cup butter in heavy large saucepan over medium-low heat. Add onion and cook until transparent, stirring occasionally, about 10 minutes. Add tomatoes with liquid and cook 10 minutes. Add remaining ½ cup butter, 2 cups stock, sugar, cinnamon, ½ teaspoon salt and pepper and bring soup to simmer, stirring occasionally.

Meanwhile, combine flour, baking powder and remaining ½ teaspoon salt in large bowl. Add eggs and oil and beat until dough is sticky. Drop dough by ½ teaspoonfuls into simmering soup; do not stir. Cover and simmer until dumplings are firm and cooked through, about 15 minutes. (If dumplings absorb too much liquid and soup is too thick, add more stock.) Garnish with bell pepper and serve immediately.

Minnesota Wild Rice Soup

6 to 8 servings

Stock

2 duck or chicken carcasses or 2½ pounds chicken necks and backs
5 cups water
1 smoked ham bone (about 8 ounces)
2 carrots, coarsely chopped
1 medium onion, sliced
¼ celery stalk, chopped
1 tablespoon Maggi seasoning or Knorr-Swiss Aromat seasoning
1 bay leaf
½ teaspoon salt
  Freshly ground pepper

Soup

¼ cup (½ stick) butter
½ cup finely chopped onion
½ cup finely chopped celery
½ cup finely chopped carrot
¼ cup uncooked wild rice or 2 cups cooked
2 tablespoons sliced blanched almonds

2 cups whipping cream
2 teaspoons arrowroot dissolved in small amount of whipping cream (optional)

For stock: Combine all ingredients in large pot and bring to boil over high heat. Reduce heat to medium-low and simmer uncovered about 1½ hours. Strain; discard all fat.

For soup: Melt butter in heavy large saucepan over medium-high heat. Add onion, celery, carrot, wild rice and almonds and sauté until vegetables are slightly softened, about 5 minutes. Add stock and bring to boil. Reduce heat to medium-low and simmer mixture for about 1¼ hours.

Just before serving, stir in cream and heat through; *do not boil.* Blend in arrowroot mixture if thicker soup is desired.

3 🍎 Breads

The nation's breadbaskets have held a profusion of regional specialties since the days of the New England colonists and their hearth-baked jonnycakes. This chapter offers a sampling of some of these special American breads. Spoon breads, corn breads, popovers, hush puppies and biscuits are traditional favorites, while Graham Granola Bread (page 24) and Pumpkin Spoon Bread (page 27) are new twists on familiar classics.

There are interesting variations on signature Southern corn breads, such as southwestern Spiced Masa Corn Muffins (page 29) and Green Chili Corn Bread (page 28). But Yankee bakers are well represented too, with such recipes as Cranberry Maple Muffins (page 32), Boston Brown Bread (page 32), and Parker House Rolls (page 26), from that same city's historic Parker House hotel.

Homemade bread makes a meal very special, even though a quick loaf or a pan of muffins can be prepared in practically no time. Remember, too, that yeast dough, or any bread that is already baked, can be made long ahead and frozen, ready to be called into service for a busy-day meal or for last-minute entertaining.

Yeast Breads

New Orleans French Bread

This is best served the day it is baked.

Makes 1 large loaf

½ cup warm water (105°F to 115°F)
1½ tablespoons dry yeast
1 teaspoon sugar

4 cups (or more) unbleached all purpose flour
2 teaspoons salt

1½ teaspoons solid vegetable shortening
¾ to 1 cup warm water (105°F to 115°F)
¼ cup cornmeal

Stir warm water, yeast and sugar in large bowl until yeast is dissolved. Proof until foamy, about 10 minutes.

Mix 4 cups flour, salt and shortening in processor using 3 to 4 on/off turns. Blend in yeast mixture using 3 to 4 on/off turns. With machine running, pour ¾ cup warm water through feed tube in slow, steady stream and process until dough just cleans side of bowl. (If dough is too wet, blend in more flour 1 tablespoon at a time. If too dry, add up to ¼ cup more warm water with machine running.) Process 60 seconds.

Turn dough out onto lightly floured surface. Knead to form dsmooth ball, 5 to 6 times. Oil large bowl. Transfer dough to bowl, turning to coat entire surface. Cover with damp towel. Let dough rise in warm draft-free area until doubled, about 1½ hours.

Punch dough down. Turn out onto lightly floured surface and roll into 10 × 15-inch rectangle. Starting with long side, roll dough up into cylinder. Tuck ends under. Pinch seam to seal. Sprinkle cornmeal on large baking sheet. Set loaf on sheet. Cover with damp towel. Let rise in warm draft-free area until doubled in volume, about 1 hour.

Preheat oven to 400°F. Using razor blade or sharp knife, make 3 diagonal slashes across top of loaf. Brush loaf with water. Bake 15 minutes; brush again with water. Reduce oven temperature to 350°F. Continue baking until loaf is golden brown and sounds hollow when tapped on bottom, about 20 minutes. Cool on rack before slicing.

Graham Granola Bread

Use your favorite granola for this deliciously healthful breakfast loaf.

Makes 2 loaves

1½ envelopes dry yeast or 1½ cakes fresh yeast
1 tablespoon sugar
½ cup warm or lukewarm water (see below)

1 cup water
1 cup buttermilk
¼ cup (½ stick) unsalted butter
¼ cup honey or firmly packed brown sugar
1¼ cups graham* or whole wheat flour

1 cup granola, finely ground in processor or blender
½ cup rolled oats
½ cup chopped walnuts
1½ teaspoons salt
1 egg, room temperature
3½ to 4½ cups unbleached all purpose flour or bread flour

Sprinkle dry yeast and sugar over ½ cup warm water (105°F to 115°F) in small bowl and stir to dissolve. If using cake yeast, crumble into small bowl. Stir in sugar and ½ cup lukewarm water (95°F). Let mixture stand until foamy, about 10 minutes.

Meanwhile, heat 1 cup water, buttermilk, butter and honey in heavy small saucepan to lukewarm (95°F), stirring until butter melts. Combine graham flour, granola, oats, walnuts and salt in large bowl. Add yeast and lukewarm liquid mixture, then egg, whisking until thick, about 5 minutes. Using wooden spoon, mix in enough all purpose flour ½ cup at a time to form soft dough. Knead on floured surface until smooth and elastic, kneading in more all purpose flour if dough is sticky.

Grease large bowl and add dough, turning to coat entire surface. Cover bowl with plastic wrap. Let dough rise in warm draft-free area until doubled in volume, about 1 hour.

Grease two 9 × 5-inch loaf pans (preferably black steel). Gently knead dough on lightly floured surface until deflated. Cut dough in half. Pat each piece out into rectangle. Roll up jelly roll fashion, pinching seams to seal. Place seam side down in prepared pans. Cover with towel. Let rise in warm draft-free area until doubled in volume, about 45 minutes.

Preheat oven to 375°F. Bake until loaves sound hollow when tapped on bottom, about 40 minutes. Immediately remove from pans. Cool completely on wire racks before slicing.

*Available at natural foods stores.

Buttermilk Yeast Biscuits

Makes about 4 dozen

1 envelope dry yeast
2 tablespoons warm water (105°F to 115°F)
5 to 5½ cups sifted all purpose flour
2 tablespoons sugar
1 tablespoon baking powder

1 teaspoon baking soda
1 teaspoon salt
1 cup solid vegetable shortening
2 cups buttermilk

Melted butter

Sprinkle yeast over warm water in small bowl and let stand until dissolved, about 5 minutes. Meanwhile, resift flour with sugar, baking powder, soda and salt into large bowl. Using pastry blender, cut in shortening until mixture resembles coarse meal. Mix in buttermilk and dissolved yeast. Turn dough out onto lightly floured work surface and knead until smooth and soft, about 10 minutes.

Position rack in upper third of oven and preheat to 450°F. Reflour work surface. Roll dough out to thickness of ½ inch. Cut out biscuits using 2-inch cutter. Transfer to ungreased baking sheet, spacing evenly. Brush tops with melted butter. Bake until lightly browned, about 15 minutes. Serve hot. (Biscuits can be baked 1 day ahead. Reheat in 450°F oven before serving.)

Golden Harvest Rolls

Makes 12

¼ cup firmly packed light brown
   sugar
1 envelope dry yeast
¼ cup warm water (105°F to 115°F)

1 large sweet potato, baked until
   very soft, cooled
3 tablespoons unsalted butter,
   room temperature

3 cups bread flour
1½ teaspoons salt
½ teaspoon ground cardamom
¾ cup milk
¾ cup golden raisins

1 egg beaten with ½ teaspoon salt
   (glaze)

Sprinkle sugar and yeast over water; stir to dissolve. Let stand until foamy and proofed, about 10 minutes.

Scoop out potato pulp. Mash with butter. Combine flour, salt and cardamom in large bowl. Mix in potato. Add yeast mixture and milk and stir until dough comes together. Turn out onto lightly floured surface and knead until smooth and elastic, about 8 minutes. Knead in raisins. Grease large bowl. Add dough, turning to coat entire surface. Cover with oiled plastic wrap and let rise in warm draft-free area until doubled, about 1 hour.

Grease twelve ⅓-cup fluted brioche molds and arrange on baking sheet. Turn dough out onto lightly floured surface and divide into 12 portions. Divide each into 2 pieces, one 3 times as large as the other. Roll both pieces into smooth rounds. Set larger round into prepared mold. Using finger, make indentation in center, then fit in smaller round. Repeat with remaining dough. Cover with oiled plastic and let rise in warm draft-free area until doubled in volume, about 1 hour.

Position rack in center of oven and preheat to 400°F. Brush tops of rolls with glaze; do not glaze seam. Bake until golden brown, about 15 minutes. Remove immediately from molds. Serve warm or at room temperature. (*Can be prepared 1 month ahead. Cool completely, flash-freeze on baking sheet, then wrap and freeze. To reheat, wrap frozen rolls loosely in foil. Bake in 400°F oven until heated through, about 25 minutes.*)

Parker House Rolls

*Makes about 5 dozen
2-inch rolls*

¼ cup warm water (105°F to 115°F)
1 envelope dry yeast
½ teaspoon sugar
⅓ cup solid vegetable shortening
¼ cup sugar
1 egg
1 teaspoon salt

1 cup warm water (105°F to 115°F)
2 cups all purpose flour

1½ to 2 cups unbleached all purpose
   flour

¾ cup (1½ sticks) butter, melted

Generously butter large bowl and large rectangular baking pan and set aside. Combine ¼ cup warm water with yeast and sugar in small bowl and stir until yeast is dissolved. Let stand until foamy and proofed, about 10 minutes. Combine shortening, sugar, egg and salt in large bowl of electric mixer and beat at medium speed until light and fluffy. With mixer running, add yeast mixture and 1 cup warm water and blend well. Gradually beat in 2 cups flour. Continue beating about 2 minutes, scraping down sides of bowl.

Insert dough hook. Slowly add 1½ cups unbleached flour to dough and knead until dough is very soft, about 5 minutes, or 10 minutes by hand. (Add more flour only as necessary; the less flour the lighter the rolls.)

Shape dough into ball and transfer to prepared bowl, turning to coat entire surface. Cover and let rise in warm draft-free area (85°F) until doubled in volume, about 2½ hours.

Punch dough down. Turn out onto lightly floured surface and knead until smooth and elastic. Cover with inverted large mixing bowl and let rest 15 minutes. Turn dough out onto lightly floured surface and roll into circle ½ inch thick. Cut dough into 2-inch circles. Dip circles into melted butter and fold in half. Arrange close together in neat rows on prepared pan. Brush rolls with melted butter. Cover pan and let rolls rise in warm draft-free area until doubled in volume, 45 to 60 minutes.

Position rack in upper third of oven and preheat to 425°F. Bake rolls until browned, about 18 to 20 minutes. Remove from oven, brush with butter and serve immediately, or let cool on rack until ready to serve.

Quick Breads

The Greenbrier's Spoon Bread

10 servings

1 quart water
1¾ cups white cornmeal
9 tablespoons butter
¼ cup sugar
2 teaspoons salt

3½ cups milk
7 eggs, beaten to blend
2 tablespoons baking powder

Bring water, cornmeal, butter, sugar and salt to boil in heavy large saucepan, stirring occasionally. Remove from heat. Whisk in milk in slow steady stream until smooth. Gradually whisk in eggs. Cool completely.

Preheat oven to 375°F. Grease 4½-quart baking dish. Blend baking powder into cornmeal mixture. Pour into prepared dish. Bake until puffed and golden, about 50 minutes. Serve immediately.

Pumpkin Spoon Bread

This slightly sweet, slightly spicy side dish is a new version of an early American favorite. It is also excellent with roast lamb, pork, sausages or ham.

4 to 6 servings

3 tablespoons butter
1 16-ounce can solid pack pumpkin
7 tablespoons sugar
1 tablespoon Hungarian sweet paprika
1 teaspoon salt
4 eggs, room temperature

⅓ cup buttermilk
1 cup stone-ground cornmeal
1 teaspoon baking powder
½ teaspoon baking soda
Butter
Freshly ground pepper

Preheat oven to 375°F. Melt 3 tablespoons butter in 6-cup soufflé dish in oven. Whisk pumpkin, sugar, paprika and salt in medium bowl. Whisk in eggs one at a time. Stir in buttermilk. Add dry ingredients and whisk until well combined. Tilt hot soufflé dish to coat bottom and sides with butter. Pour in pumpkin mixture. Bake until puffed and light brown, about 40 minutes. Serve immediately, passing butter and pepper separately.

Green Chili Corn Bread

8 servings

2 eggs
¼ cup sugar
1 cup plain yogurt
1 cup all purpose flour
1 cup cornmeal
2 teaspoons baking powder
1 teaspoon baking soda
½ cup frozen whole kernel corn, thawed and drained

1 4-ounce can chopped mild green chilies, drained
¼ cup (½ stick) butter, cut into 4 pieces, room temperature
1 tablespoon finely chopped red bell pepper

Preheat oven to 425°F. Butter 9-inch square baking dish. Beat eggs and sugar in large bowl. Stir in yogurt. Combine flour, cornmeal, baking powder and baking soda in medium bowl. Blend into yogurt mixture. Add corn, chilies and butter and mix well. Turn into prepared baking dish. Sprinkle with red pepper. Bake until bread is golden and toothpick inserted in center comes out clean, 15 to 20 minutes. Serve immediately.

Mile-High Popovers

Try filling these with a savory meat or vegetable mixture for a main dish, or with dessert sauces and whipped cream to top off an evening meal. They are also delicious served warm with maple syrup and butter for a quick hot breakfast.

6 servings

1 cup milk
2 eggs

1 cup sifted all purpose flour
½ teaspoon salt

Grease 6 custard cups and arrange on baking sheet. Combine milk and eggs in medium bowl and mix well. Gradually whisk in flour and salt until flour is well incorporated; batter may be lumpy. Fill each cup ¾ full. Place baking sheet in cold oven, then turn temperature to 425°F. Bake 30 minutes; *do not open oven door.* Let popovers stand in oven 10 minutes. Loosen popovers from cups and turn out onto racks. Serve immediately.

Popovers can be frozen. Thaw and reheat on baking sheet in 350°F oven for about 5 minutes.

Yorkshire Pudding Popovers

Cast-iron muffin tins yield the crispest and highest popovers.

Makes 16

2 cups all purpose flour
2 cups extra-rich milk
4 eggs, room temperature
1 teaspoon salt
½ teaspoon sugar

Vegetable oil
8 to 16 teaspoons beef fat drippings (see recipe for Plymouth Prime Rib, page 34)

Mix flour, milk, eggs, salt and sugar in processor or blender until very smooth. Cover and chill 1 to 2 hours.

Preheat oven to 400°F. Grease muffin tins with vegetable oil. Melt beef fat drippings. Place ½ to 1 teaspoon drippings in each muffin cup. Rebeat batter until smooth, then fill each cup ⅔ full with batter. Bake 15 minutes; do not open oven door. Reduce oven temperature to 375°F and continue baking until popovers are golden brown, 15 to 20 minutes. Immediately slash each popover on side to allow steam to escape. Turn oven off. Let popovers cool 5 minutes in oven with door ajar. Serve immediately.

Corn Popovers

6 servings

⅓ cup fresh or frozen thawed corn
    kernels
⅓ cup (or more) water
2 eggs, beaten to blend
½ cup milk

1 tablespoon vegetable oil
1 teaspoon sugar
½ teaspoon salt
    Pinch of freshly ground pepper
1 cup all purpose flour

Preheat oven to 425°F. Generously grease six 6-ounce custard cups. Mince corn with ⅓ cup water in blender. Drain corn through sieve into measuring cup. Add more water if necessary to measure ½ cup liquid. Mix corn liquid, eggs, milk, oil, sugar, salt and pepper in medium bowl. Whisk in flour until smooth. Stir in corn. Place prepared custard cups on baking sheet. Heat in oven 4 minutes. Remove from oven and ladle ⅓ cup batter into each cup. Bake 15 minutes. Reduce oven temperature to 400°F. Continue baking until firm and brown, about 20 minutes. Carefully remove popovers from cups; pierce with knife. Turn popovers on sides. Place on baking sheet. Bake until crisp and dry, about 5 minutes. Serve immediately.

The Inn at Chester Corn Sticks

Makes about 2 dozen

1½ cups bread flour
1½ cups cornmeal
½ cup sugar
1½ teaspoons salt
1½ teaspoons baking soda

2 cups buttermilk
¾ cup (1½ sticks) butter, melted
    and cooled
2 eggs, well beaten
½ cup corn kernels

Preheat oven to 400°F. Place corn stick molds in oven. Mix flour, cornmeal, sugar, salt and baking soda in large bowl. Add buttermilk, butter and eggs and stir until smooth. Blend in corn. Spoon into hot molds. Bake until golden brown, about 10 minutes. Serve immediately.

Spiced Masa Corn Muffins

Makes 8

2 tablespoons fresh parsley leaves
1 cup unbleached all purpose flour
¾ cup plain yogurt
½ cup vegetable oil
7 tablespoons yellow instant masa
    mix or yellow cornmeal
2 eggs
¼ cup sugar
2 teaspoons baking powder

1 teaspoon dried red pepper flakes
½ teaspoon ground coriander
½ teaspoon baking soda
½ teaspoon salt
    Butter

Position rack in center of oven and preheat to 375°F. Generously grease eight ½-cup muffin cups.

    Mince parsley in food processor. Add all remaining ingredients except butter and process 3 seconds, stopping once to scrape down sides of work bowl. Continue processing until just mixed, about 1 more second. Divide batter among prepared muffin cups. Bake until light brown, 20 to 25 minutes. Cool in pan 8 minutes. Serve muffins warm with butter.

Ann Elizabeth's Hush Puppies

For a variation, replace the jalapeño pepper with ¾ cup chopped green onions.

6 to 8 servings

1 cup yellow cornmeal
¼ cup all purpose flour
1½ tablespoons sugar
1 jalapeño pepper, seeded and minced
1 teaspoon baking powder
½ teaspoon salt

9 tablespoons boiling water
1 egg, beaten to blend

Vegetable oil (for deep frying)
Butter

Combine first 6 ingredients in bowl. Mix in boiling water and egg.

Heat oil in deep fryer or large saucepan to 350°F. Drop 1½-inch balls of batter into oil in batches (do not crowd) and fry until golden brown, turning occasionally, about 1 minute. Transfer to paper towels to drain, using slotted spoon. Serve immediately with butter.

Stagecoach Inn Sweet Hush Puppies

Makes about 32

2½ cups water
¾ cup (1½ sticks) butter
2 cups plus 2 tablespoons white cornmeal
½ cup (scant) sugar

1 tablespoon salt
1½ teaspoons baking powder

Oil (for deep frying)

Combine water and butter in large saucepan and bring to rolling boil over high heat. Blend dry ingredients in medium bowl. Remove butter mixture from heat. Fold in dry ingredients. Let cool slightly. Form into 2-inch balls.

Heat oil in saucepan or deep fryer to 350°F. Add hush puppies in small batches and fry, turning once, until browned, about 2 minutes per side, keeping oil temperature constant. Drain on paper towels. Serve hot.

Herbed Buttermilk Biscuits

For the lightest and flakiest biscuits, handle dough as little as possible.

Makes 20

3 cups all purpose flour
⅓ cup sugar
2 tablespoons baking powder
1 teaspoon salt
1 teaspoon baking soda
½ cup solid vegetable shortening
½ cup (1 stick) well-chilled butter, cut into small pieces

3 tablespoons unsalted butter
1 small onion, minced

⅓ cup minced celery leaves
2 tablespoons minced fresh dill
2 tablespoons minced fresh parsley
2 teaspoons minced fresh thyme
2 small garlic cloves, minced

⅔ cup buttermilk
¼ cup whipping cream
Lemon-Chive Butter*

Sift together flour, sugar, baking powder, salt and baking soda. Cut in shortening and ½ cup butter until mixture resembles coarse meal. Cover and refrigerate several hours or overnight.

Melt 3 tablespoons butter in heavy medium skillet over medium heat. Add onion and stir until pale golden, about 5 minutes. Add celery leaves, dill, parsley, thyme and garlic and stir 4 minutes to blend flavors. Let mixture cool to room temperature.

Position rack in center of oven and preheat to 400°F. Line baking sheets with parchment or grease lightly. Fluff flour mixture with fork. Stir in onion mixture. Make well in center. Add buttermilk to well. Stir just until dough comes together. Turn dough out onto lightly floured surface and knead 3 times. Shape into rectangle. Using floured rolling pin, roll dough out to thickness of ½ inch. Using floured 2½-inch heart-shaped or round cutter or glass, cut out 20 biscuits. Arrange biscuits 1 inch apart on prepared sheets. Brush tops with cream. Bake until puffed and golden brown, about 15 minutes. Let cool 5 minutes on wire rack. Serve warm with lemon-chive butter.

*Lemon-Chive Butter

Although this butter is meant to be spread on the biscuits, it is also splendid on toast, baked potatoes, roast chicken and freshly made pasta.

Makes about 2¼ cups

6 tablespoons chopped fresh parsley
3 tablespoons snipped fresh chives
2 tablespoons chopped fresh tarragon
1 teaspoon grated lemon peel
2 cups (4 sticks) unsalted butter, room temperature
1 tablespoon fresh lemon juice
¼ to ½ teaspoon salt

Finely mince herbs and lemon peel in processor, scraping down sides of bowl often. Add butter, lemon juice and salt and blend well. Turn into crock. Cover tightly and chill overnight or up to 3 days. Let stand at room temperature for 30 minutes before serving.

Cinnamon Logs

From the Williamsburg Lodge in Williamsburg, Virginia.

6 servings

1 1-pound loaf unsliced firm white bread, crusts trimmed

2 cups milk
5 eggs, beaten
2 tablespoons sugar
½ to ¾ teaspoon cinnamon
½ teaspoon vanilla
Pinch of freshly grated nutmeg

Oil (for deep frying)
Whipped butter and maple syrup
6 lemon twists (optional garnish)

Cut bread into 4 × 2 × 2-inch rectangular logs. Let stand to dry slightly.

Blend milk, eggs, sugar, cinnamon, vanilla and nutmeg in medium bowl. Pour into shallow pan large enough to hold bread in 1 layer. Arrange bread in milk mixture, turning to coat all sides. Refrigerate until liquid is absorbed, several hours or overnight.

Heat oil to 360°F. Fry logs in batches until golden brown on all sides, about 3 to 4 minutes. Drain on paper towels. Serve immediately with whipped butter and maple syrup. Garnish with lemon if desired.

Carrot Bran Muffins

Makes 10

1 cup bran flakes cereal, crushed
1 cup all purpose flour
¼ cup firmly packed light brown sugar
2 teaspoons baking powder
½ teaspoon baking soda
½ teaspoon salt
½ teaspoon cinnamon
¼ teaspoon freshly grated nutmeg
1 cup milk
1 egg
3 tablespoons vegetable oil
1 cup grated carrots
¼ cup chopped walnuts
¼ cup raisins

Preheat oven to 400°F. Generously grease muffin tins. Combine first 8 ingredients in large bowl. Blend milk, egg and oil. Stir into dry ingredients just until evenly moistened. Stir in carrots, walnuts and raisins. Spoon batter into prepared tins. Bake muffins until golden and toothpick inserted in centers comes out clean, about 15 minutes. Remove from tins. Cool slightly on racks. Serve warm.

Cranberry Maple Muffins

Makes 12

1½ cups unbleached all purpose flour
½ cup walnuts
2 teaspoons baking powder
½ teaspoon salt

1½ cups cranberries

1 cup sugar

2 eggs
½ cup (1 stick) unsalted butter, cut into 4 pieces, room temperature
½ cup buttermilk
2 teaspoons maple flavoring

Position rack in center of oven and preheat to 375°F. Generously grease twelve ½-cup muffin cups; dust with flour, shaking out excess.

Blend 1½ cups flour, walnuts, baking powder and salt in food processor until nuts are coarsely chopped, about 5 seconds. Transfer to medium bowl.

Insert medium slicer into processor. Place cranberries in feed tube and slice using light pressure. Add to dry ingredients.

Reinsert steel knife. Process sugar and eggs 1 minute, stopping once to scrape down sides of work bowl. Add butter and blend until smooth, about 1 minute. With machine running, pour buttermilk and maple flavoring through feed tube and mix 10 seconds. Add dry ingredients. Blend using 2 on/off turns. Run spatula around inside of work bowl to loosen mixture. Blend until just combined, using 1 or 2 on/off turns. Spoon ⅓ cup batter into each muffin cup. Bake until light brown and springy to touch, 27 to 30 minutes. Immediately remove muffins from pan and transfer to rack. (*Can be prepared 1 day ahead. Cool completely, wrap airtight and store at room temperature. To reheat, place on greased baking sheet in cold oven. Turn oven to 350°F and warm through, about 12 minutes.*) Serve warm or at room temperature.

Boston Brown Bread

Makes 3 or 4 loaves

2 cups graham flour
2 cups buttermilk
1 cup raisins
½ cup unbleached all purpose flour

½ cup molasses
2 teaspoons baking soda
1 teaspoon salt

Lightly grease three or four 1-pound cans (4¼ inches high). Combine all ingredients and mix well. Fill cans no more than ⅔ full. Let stand 30 minutes. Preheat oven to 350°F. Bake until tester inserted in center of loaves comes out clean, about 45 to 50 minutes. Let stand until cans are cool enough to handle. Remove bottom with can opener, run knife around inside and gently push out bread. Serve warm.

4 ❦ Meats

Americans have always been devoted to meat of all kinds, with steaks, chops and roasts occupying center stage for family and company dinners alike. While this is changing somewhat, with meat no longer considered a requirement at every meal, there is little doubt that beef, pork, ham and other meats will always be among our favorite foods.

If there is one typically American method of meat preparation, it must be barbecuing. Whether cooked on an outdoor grill or oven-roasted with just the right hot and spicy seasonings, barbecued meat is unparalleled for aroma and succulence. The selection here includes both indoor and outdoor methods: Barbecued Beef Brisket (page 34), Chili-Smoked Pork (page 41), and Barbecued Pork Ribs with Sam's Special Sauce (page 42) are mesquite-grilled for deep-down smoky flavor, while "Baltimore and Ohio" Ribs and Oven-Barbecued Short Ribs with Chili Biscuits (both on page 36) bypass the outdoor grilling step and are easy to fix whatever the season or weather.

Of course, barbecuing is not the whole story. The recipe for Plymouth Prime Rib (page 34) gives the perfect method of roasting this exquisitely tender cut of beef. One-dish Creole specialties such as Saturday Night Jambalaya and Red Beans and Rice with Smoked Sausage (both on page 43) offer tantalizing tastes of Louisiana's unique cuisine. Chicken-Fried Steak with Cream Gravy (page 35) is a famed Southern classic—and so on. Whether slow-roasted or quickly seared, an inexpensive brisket or a choice hickory-smoked country ham, hearty meat dishes are central to American cooking.

Beef and Veal

Plymouth Prime Rib

A foolproof method of attaining beef with a crisp golden exterior and juicy interior. Have your butcher remove the chine bone at the base of the ribs, then have the bone tied back onto the roast to facilitate carving even slices. After roasting, save the drippings for Yorkshire Pudding Popovers (page 28) and Winter Vinaigrette (page 86).

10 servings

1 10-pound standing rib of beef (about 4 large ribs), room temperature
Vegetable oil
1 tablespoon coarse salt
1 tablespoon all purpose flour
2 teaspoons dried thyme, crumbled

¼ to ½ teaspoon freshly ground pepper
1 cup dry red wine or ale
2 cups rich beef stock, preferably homemade
Salt

Preheat oven to 500°F. Pat meat dry. Rub oil onto portions of meat not protected with fat. Combine salt, flour, thyme and pepper to taste and rub onto fat. Place meat rib side down in roasting pan just large enough to accommodate. Roast 15 minutes. Reduce oven to 350°F and roast 15 minutes per pound for rare (or until thermometer inserted in thickest part of meat without touching bone registers 130°F) or 20 minutes per pound for medium rare (or until thermometer registers 135°F to 140°F). Let stand 20 minutes before carving.

Meanwhile, pour off drippings from roasting pan. Reserve 6 to 8 tablespoons for popovers and 1 tablespoon for vinaigrette. Degrease remaining drippings; reserve 3 tablespoons for vinaigrette. Add wine to pan, scraping up browned bits, and boil until reduced to about ⅓ cup. Add stock, scraping up browned bits, and boil until thickened, about 10 minutes. Strain into sauceboat. Season with salt and pepper. Carve meat into ½-inch-thick slices. Pass sauce separately.

Sam's Rib Eye Roast

An easy but elegant main course.

12 to 20 servings

Freshly ground pepper
Garlic powder
1 8- to 12-pound boneless rib eye

roast or Spencer roast, room temperature

Preheat oven to 500°F. Rub generous amounts of pepper and garlic powder into roast. Set roast on rack in baking pan. Pour in enough water to come ½ inch up sides of pan. Roast meat 5 minutes per pound. Turn off heat; do not open oven. Let meat stand in oven 2 hours. Cut into slices and serve.

Barbecued Beef Brisket

8 servings

6 cups mesquite chips

1 4-pound beef brisket, untrimmed

2 tablespoons Dry Rub*

Barbecue Sauce**

Soak mesquite chips in water to cover for 1 hour. Drain well.

Prepare barbecue grill, lighting fire at one end only. Rub brisket with dry rub. When coals are white, place meat over coals and sear 5 minutes on each side. Move meat to side of grill away from fire. Spread 4 cups mesquite over coals. Cover grill. Smoke brisket 1 hour, maintaining temperature at about 200°F and sprinkling mesquite with water occasionally. Spread remaining 2 cups mesquite over coals and continue smoking meat 1 hour.

Preheat oven to 200°F. Cut ¹/₂ cup fat from brisket and reserve for Barbecue Sauce (see recipe below). Wrap beef tightly with heavy-duty foil. Bake 8 hours. Slice meat across grain. Serve hot. Pass barbecue sauce separately.

*Dry Rub

Makes about ¹/₄ cup

¹/₄ **cup salt**
1¹/₂ **teaspoons freshly ground pepper**

1¹/₂ **teaspoons cayenne pepper**

Mix all ingredients in small bowl.

**Barbecue Sauce

A spicy red sauce that is perfect with the barbecued beef brisket.

Makes about 2 cups

¹/₂ **cup beef fat reserved from Barbecued Beef Brisket (see recipe above)**
1¹/₄ **cups catsup**
¹/₂ **cup Worcestershire sauce**
¹/₃ **cup fresh lemon juice**

¹/₄ **cup firmly packed brown sugar**
¹/₄ **cup chopped onion**
¹/₄ **cup water**
1 **tablespoon hot pepper sauce**

Cut fat into ¹/₂-inch pieces. Heat in heavy small skillet over low heat until rendered, stirring frequently, about 30 minutes. Transfer ¹/₄ cup melted fat to heavy medium saucepan. Stir in remaining ingredients and cook over low heat until thick, about 1 hour. Serve sauce hot or warm.

Chicken-Fried Steak with Cream Gravy

Serve this steak with buttered mashed potatoes.

8 to 10 servings

1 **3-pound sirloin tip roast, cut into ¹/₂-inch slices**
1 **to 2 tablespoons salt**
1 **tablespoon distilled white vinegar**

3 **cups all purpose flour**
2 **tablespoons freshly ground pepper**
Vegetable oil (for deep frying)

Cream Gravy
2 **tablespoons all purpose flour**
1 **cup milk**
¹/₄ **teaspoon salt**
Parsley sprigs

Pound meat with spiked meat mallet to tenderize. Cut each slice crosswise into 3 pieces. Place in large bowl. Cover with water. Mix in salt and vinegar and let marinate for 2 hours.

Combine flour and pepper in plastic bag. Add meat (do not pat dry) 1 piece at a time and shake to coat. Heat oil in deep fryer or deep large skillet over medium-high heat to 350°F. Add meat in batches (do not crowd) and fry until light brown, about 30 seconds per side. Drain on paper towels. Place meat on warm platter. Tent with foil.

For gravy: Pour off all but 2 tablespoons oil in skillet, leaving browned bits. Heat over medium heat. Add flour and stir 3 minutes, scraping up any browned bits. Remove from heat and gradually whisk in milk. Stir in salt. Whisk over medium heat until thickened, about 1 minute. Spoon over steaks. Garnish with parsley sprigs and serve.

"Baltimore and Ohio" Barbecued Beef Ribs

6 servings

4 cups chili sauce
½ cup fresh lemon juice
½ cup firmly packed dark brown sugar
3 tablespoons Worcestershire sauce
1 tablespoon hot pepper sauce
1 tablespoon paprika

1 teaspoon salt
1 teaspoon freshly ground pepper

18 roasted beef ribs or braised short ribs (or combination)

Combine chili sauce, lemon juice, sugar, Worcestershire sauce, hot pepper sauce, paprika, salt and pepper in large saucepan and bring to boil. Reduce heat and simmer 15 to 20 minutes, stirring occasionally.

Preheat oven to 350°F. Arrange ribs in single layer in large shallow roasting pan. Cover each rib with ¼ cup sauce. Bake until ribs are crisp, about 25 minutes. Serve immediately.

Oven-Barbecued Short Ribs with Chili Biscuits

6 to 8 servings

3 pounds beef short ribs, cut into 1-inch pieces

3 tablespoons vegetable oil
2 large onions, coarsely chopped
4 large garlic cloves, minced
2 16-ounce cans tomatoes, undrained
2 cups beef stock
⅓ cup cider vinegar
¼ cup firmly packed light brown sugar
3 tablespoons Worcestershire sauce
2 tablespoons Dijon mustard
1½ teaspoons salt
1½ teaspoons cayenne pepper*
½ teaspoon freshly ground pepper
½ teaspoon paprika
½ teaspoon turmeric
10 parsley sprigs, tied together
2 ¼-inch-thick lemon slices

1 pound medium boiling potatoes, peeled and cut into 1-inch cubes
1 pound medium carrots, cut into 2-inch pieces

Chili Biscuits
1 tablespoon unsalted butter
1 medium onion, minced
1 large garlic clove, minced

2 cups sifted all purpose flour
1 tablespoon baking powder
2 teaspoons chili powder
1 teaspoon salt
¼ cup freshly grated Parmesan cheese
2 tablespoons minced fresh cilantro or parsley
⅓ cup well-chilled lard or solid vegetable shortening
¾ cup milk

Preheat broiler. Arrange ribs in single layer in large shallow roasting pan. Broil 4 inches from heat until brown, turning frequently, about 10 minutes.

Preheat oven to 350°F. Heat oil in Dutch oven over medium-low heat. Add onions and garlic and cook until soft and golden brown, stirring frequently, about 10 minutes. Add ribs and any drippings. Stir in tomatoes, stock, vinegar, sugar, Worcestershire, mustard, salt, cayenne, pepper, paprika, turmeric, parsley and lemon. Increase heat and bring to boil. Transfer to oven, cover and bake until short ribs are just tender, about 2 hours.

Stir potatoes and carrots into ribs. Cover and bake until vegetables are tender, about 40 minutes. Discard parsley and lemon. Degrease sauce. Adjust seasoning. (*Can be prepared 3 days ahead, covered and refrigerated or prepared 1 month ahead and frozen. Bring to simmer before continuing with recipe.*)

For biscuits: Melt butter in heavy small skillet over medium-low heat. Add onion and garlic and cook until soft, stirring occasionally, about 10 minutes. Cool mixture 10 minutes.

Sift flour, baking powder, chili powder and salt into large bowl. Stir in cheese and cilantro. Cut in lard with pastry blender until mixture resembles coarse meal. Blend in onion mixture. Make well in center of flour mixture. Add milk to well and mix with fork just until dough comes together. Turn dough out onto lightly floured surface and knead 3 to 5 times. Roll dough out to ½-inch thickness. Cut out biscuits using 3-inch floured cutter.

Increase oven temperature to 450°F. Arrange biscuits over ribs. Bake uncovered until biscuits are puffed and lightly browned, about 15 minutes. Serve short ribs immediately.

*Increase cayenne pepper to 2 teaspoons if mixture is to be frozen.

Cheddar Burgers

Makes 8

8 ounces sharp cheddar cheese, chilled and cut into 1-inch cubes
2 pounds lean beef, cut into 1-inch cubes and chilled
8 ounces beef fat, cut into 1-inch cubes and chilled
¼ cup ice water *or* 1 egg, beaten to blend

3 teaspoons Worcestershire sauce
1½ teaspoons salt
Freshly ground pepper

Hamburger rolls

Finely chop cheese in food processor. Remove from work bowl. Combine ⅓ of beef with ⅓ of fat and chop finely, about 20 seconds. Add ⅓ of cheese, 4 teaspoons water, 1 teaspoon Worcestershire, ½ teaspoon salt and pinch of pepper. Mix until cheese is evenly distributed, about 5 seconds. Remove from processor work bowl. Repeat with remaining ingredients in 2 batches. Gently form into 8 patties.

Prepare barbecue grill; oil rack. Cook patties to desired degree of doneness 4 to 6 inches from heat, turning once. Serve with hamburger rolls.

Jean's Chili

Very long, slow simmering makes for full flavor and exceptionally tender meat.

10 to 12 servings

1 pound bacon, chopped
2 pounds coarsely ground round steak
½ cup chili powder
1 teaspoon salt
4 large onions, chopped
2 16-ounce cans diced tomatoes, undrained
½ teaspoon baking soda

2 15-ounce cans pinto beans, undrained
3 whole large dried red chilies
3 garlic cloves
1¼ tablespoons cumin
1 tablespoon Worcestershire sauce

Divide bacon between 2 heavy large skillets and fry over medium heat until crisp. Remove bacon with slotted spoon and drain on paper towels; do not clean skillets. Brown beef with chili powder and salt in 1 skillet over medium-high heat. Sauté onions in other skillet over medium heat until transparent, about 20 minutes. Combine tomatoes with liquid and baking soda in heavy large saucepan and bring to boil over high heat. Add beans with liquid, red chilies, garlic, cumin and Worcestershire. Stir in bacon, beef and onions. Reduce heat to low, cover and simmer 5 hours, stirring occasionally. Cool completely. Refrigerate, covered, at least 8 hours or overnight.

Simmer chili over low heat, covered, stirring occasionally, 7 more hours. Remove dried red chilies and garlic and discard. Ladle chili into bowls and serve.

True Texas Chili

If it is available, try substituting ground fresh venison for ground beef.

Makes about 8 cups

2 tablespoons vegetable oil
2 pounds lean ground beef
2 medium onions, chopped (about 2 cups)
2 garlic cloves, finely chopped
1 28-ounce can whole tomatoes
1 12-ounce can beer
5 tablespoons chili powder
2 jalapeño peppers, seeded and chopped

1 tablespoon cumin
2 teaspoons paprika
1 teaspoon sugar
Salt and freshly ground pepper
Cayenne pepper (optional)
Shredded cheddar cheese, chopped red onion and sliced avocado (optional garnishes)

Heat oil in 6-quart saucepan. Add ground beef, onions and garlic and sauté until meat is browned. Stir in next 7 ingredients and bring to boil over medium-high heat. Reduce heat to medium-low and simmer, uncovered, about 45 to 55 minutes. Taste and season with salt, pepper and cayenne, if desired. Ladle into bowls. Garnish with cheese, onion and avocado.

Boardinghouse Meat Pie

Definitely from a four-star boardinghouse. The flaky pastry can be used with any main-course pie; or cut into rounds, add your favorite filling and fold in half for hors d'oeuvres.

8 servings

1 tablespoon butter
2 cups minced onion
8 ounces mushrooms, coarsely chopped
2 pounds lean ground beef, pork or combination
¼ cup dry red wine
2 slices white bread, crumbled
2 teaspoons salt

½ teaspoon freshly ground pepper
½ teaspoon dried thyme, crumbled
8 ounces cream cheese, diced
¾ cup minced fresh parsley

1 egg yolk beaten with 1 tablespoon water (glaze)
Onion Pastry*

Melt butter in heavy large skillet over medium-low heat. Add onion and cook until soft, stirring frequently, about 10 minutes. Add mushrooms and meat. Increase heat to high and stir until meat is no longer pink. Add wine and stir until all liquid evaporates, about 8 minutes. Stir in bread, salt, pepper and thyme. Blend in cream cheese and parsley. Cool to room temperature. (*Can be prepared 1 day ahead and refrigerated. Bring to room temperature before continuing.*)

Position rack in center of oven and preheat to 400°F. Spoon meat into 10-inch pie plate. Brush upper edge and outer rim of plate with glaze. Roll larger piece of onion pastry out on lightly floured surface to 12-inch circle. Cut small hole in center. Place dough over filling, centering steam hole. Press overhanging dough firmly to edge of plate. Press tines of fork along rim. Roll remaining dough out ¼ inch thick. Cut out decorative shapes. Brush pie with glaze. Bake until golden brown, about 40 minutes. Cool pie for 10 minutes before serving.

*Onion Pastry

2 **cups all purpose flour**	¾ **cup (1½ sticks) well-chilled**
3 **tablespoons dried onion flakes**	**butter, cut into 12 pieces**
1 **teaspoon salt**	1 **egg**
1 **teaspoon sugar**	2 **to 4 tablespoons ice water**
¼ **teaspoon freshly ground pepper**	

Blend dry ingredients in processor. Cut in butter using on/off turns until mixture resembles coarse meal. With machine running, add egg and 2 tablespoons water through feed tube; blend until dough begins to gather together. Add remaining water a little at a time if dough is dry. Gather dough together. Cut off 2-inch round. Form both pieces into rounds; flatten into discs. Wrap tightly and refrigerate 30 minutes. (*Can be prepared 3 days ahead.*)

Mamete's Grillades and Grits

*A New Orleans
Creole classic.*

4 to 6 servings

2 **teaspoons salt**
1 **teaspoon freshly ground pepper**
¼ **teaspoon cayenne pepper**
4 **or 5 garlic cloves, minced**

1½ **to 1¾ pounds veal or beef round, well trimmed and cut into 2-inch squares**
All purpose flour

2 **tablespoons (¼ stick) unsalted butter**
1 **tablespoon vegetable oil**
2 **cups water**
1½ **cups chopped onion**

½ **cup finely chopped celery**
½ **cup finely chopped green bell pepper**
6 **tablespoons tomato paste**
¼ **teaspoon dried thyme, crumbled**
Salt and freshly ground pepper
Hot pepper sauce
1 **tablespoon vinegar (optional)**

2 **cups freshly cooked grits**
¼ **cup (½ stick) unsalted butter**
1 **egg**
Salt

½ **cup finely chopped green onion**

Mix first 4 ingredients in small bowl.

Using tenderizer mallet, pound each piece of meat until slightly flattened. Dip mallet into garlic mixture and then pound into the meat (1 dip per side). When meat has spread to double its original size, rub each side with a little flour.

Heat 2 tablespoons butter and oil in Dutch oven over medium-high heat. Add meat in batches and sauté until browned. Transfer to platter. Add water, onion, celery, green pepper, tomato paste, and thyme to Dutch oven and cook, stirring constantly, until vegetables are tender. Return meat to pot and season with salt, pepper and pepper sauce to taste. Cover and simmer until meat is tender, about 1 hour. (*Tenderizing can be hastened by adding vinegar when meat is returned to pot. Stir through to blend well.*)

Combine grits, butter and egg and blend well. Season to taste with salt.

Stir green onion into grillades. Spoon grits onto heated serving plates and top with grillades. Serve immediately.

Sliced Liver and Onions

4 servings

2 tablespoons fresh parsley leaves
1 small garlic clove

2 medium onions (4 ounces each), halved

2 tablespoons oil (preferably peanut)
12 ounces beef or calf's liver, sliced into 4 pieces

¼ teaspoon sugar
1 tablespoon dry Sherry
¾ teaspoon salt
Freshly ground pepper

Mince parsley in food processor using on/off turns. Transfer to small bowl and set aside for garnish. Mince garlic by dropping through feed tube with machine running. Transfer to another bowl.

Insert thin slicer into processor. Slice onions using firm pressure. Remove from work bowl and set aside.

Heat 1 tablespoon oil in large skillet over high heat. Add liver and garlic and sauté until liver is partially browned with some rosy spots. Transfer to plate and set aside.

Heat remaining oil in another skillet over medium-high heat. Add onions and sugar and sauté until onion is golden. Add liver, Sherry, salt and pepper and stir until heated through; *do not overcook liver.* Taste and adjust seasonings. Transfer to serving platter and garnish with reserved parsley.

Veal La Louisiane

4 servings

4 2½-ounce slices boneless veal
Salt and freshly ground white pepper
All purpose flour
2 tablespoons vegetable oil
8 ounces mushrooms, sliced
2 cups whipping cream
¼ cup Madeira

¼ cup (½ stick) butter, cut into 12 pieces
4 ounces cooked crabmeat
8 jumbo shrimp, peeled, deveined and cooked
4 poached crayfish (optional)

Pound veal to thickness of ¼ inch. Season with salt and pepper. Dredge lightly in flour, shaking off excess. Heat oil in large skillet over medium heat. Add veal and brown 45 seconds on each side. Transfer veal to platter and keep warm. Add mushrooms to skillet and sauté 5 minutes. Add cream and Madeira and reduce until thickened, about 15 minutes. Season with salt and pepper. Stir in ¼ cup butter 1 piece at a time, incorporating each piece completely before adding next. Add crabmeat and shrimp and heat through, about 1 minute. Pour over veal. Top each slice with 1 poached crayfish if desired. Serve immediately.

🍎 *Pork, Ham and Sausage*

Sam's Chili

Long simmering brings out the good flavors of this chili. It is best reheated and served the day after it is cooked.

6 to 8 servings

1½ pounds beef chuck roast, coarsely ground
1½ pounds pork shoulder, cut into ½-inch cubes
1 large onion, chopped
3 large garlic cloves, minced
3 cups beer or water
1 cup Special Tomatoes*
1 8-ounce can tomato sauce

½ cup chili powder
1 tablespoon salt
1 tablespoon cumin
1½ teaspoons paprika

2 tablespoons instant masa mix combined with 3 tablespoons warm water

Stir both meats, onion and garlic in heavy large saucepan or Dutch oven over medium heat until meat is no longer pink. Mix in beer, then all remaining ingredients except masa. Cover and simmer until chili is reduced to 12 cups, stirring occasionally, about 3 hours.

Degrease chili. Stir dissolved masa into chili. Cover and simmer 30 minutes. Refrigerate overnight to blend flavors. (*Can be prepared 5 days ahead.*)

*Special Tomatoes

Makes about 1 cup

1½ pounds tomatoes, peeled and coarsely chopped
1 serrano or jalapeño pepper, minced

¾ teaspoon salt
¼ teaspoon freshly ground pepper

Combine all ingredients in heavy small saucepan over medium heat. Cook 10 minutes, stirring occasionally.

Chili-Smoked Pork

This savory dish can be prepared in a smoker or covered barbecue.

8 to 10 servings

Marinade
1 12-ounce jar chili sauce
1 7-ounce can diced green chilies
1 teaspoon hot pepper sauce
½ to 1 small jalapeño pepper, seeded and chopped

2 3½-pound boneless pork rib end roasts, rolled and tied
1 12-ounce can beer

1 cup mesquite chips, soaked in water to cover 30 minutes and drained
Sliced tomatoes, watercress and green onions

For marinade: Combine first 4 ingredients in medium bowl.

Rub marinade thoroughly into pork, pushing some into pocket. Arrange in roasting pan. Pour in beer. Refrigerate 24 hours, turning occasionally.

Preheat coals to medium-low in smoker.* Spread mesquite on coals. Pour marinade into drip pan and fill with water. Arrange pork on smoker rack over drip pan. Cover smoker and smoke until thermometer inserted in thickest part of meat registers 170°F, adding more water to drip pan if necessary to keep full, about 5½ hours. Set pork on platter and surround with tomatoes, watercress and green onions. Serve warm or at room temperature.

*To smoke pork in covered barbecue, preheat coals to medium-low in barbecue grill. Push coals to sides. Place marinade in 7 × 11-inch disposable aluminum pan. Place in center of coals and fill with water. Spread mesquite over coals. Smoke pork until thermometer inserted in thickest part registers 170°F, turning several times.

Barbecued Pork Ribs with Sam's Special Sauce

8 servings

1½ quarts mesquite chips

¼ cup Dry Rub (see recipe with Barbecued Beef Brisket, page 35)

12 pounds pork spareribs (do not separate ribs)

Sam's Special Sauce*

Soak mesquite chips in water to cover for 30 minutes. Drain well.

Prepare barbecue grill, lighting fire at one end only. When coals turn white, spread ⅓ of mesquite over coals. Rub dry rub into ribs. Place on grill away from fire. Cover and smoke 3 hours, maintaining temperature at about 275°F and turning ribs every hour; add more mesquite every hour and sprinkle chips with water occasionally.

Baste smoked ribs with sauce. Cover and cook until very tender, basting and turning occasionally, about 1½ hours. Cut ribs apart and serve hot.

*Sam's Special Sauce

Makes about 3 cups

2 cups prepared mustard
½ cup beer
½ cup firmly packed light brown sugar

2½ teaspoons hot pepper sauce

Combine all ingredients. (*Can be prepared 3 days ahead and refrigerated.*)

Greek Pork and Collards

The mother of Savannah's mayor John Rousakis was a Greek immigrant. She created this version of collards, tomatoes and pork spareribs.

4 servings

2 tablespoons (¼ stick) butter
2 tablespoons olive oil
2 pounds pork spareribs, cut crosswise into 1-inch pieces and patted dry
1 large onion, chopped
1 14½-ounce can tomatoes, undrained

1 teaspoon sugar
3 pounds collard greens, stemmed
   Salt and freshly ground pepper

Melt butter with oil in heavy Dutch oven over medium-high heat. Brown spareribs on all sides. Reduce heat to low. Add onion, cover and cook until translucent, stirring frequently, about 10 minutes. Mix in tomatoes and sugar and bring to boil. Arrange collard greens atop ribs. Season with salt and pepper. Cover and simmer 10 minutes. Stir greens into liquid. Cover and simmer until collards and ribs are tender, about 45 minutes. Adjust seasoning. Serve immediately. (*Can be prepared several hours ahead. Reheat before serving.*)

Sautéed Pork Chops with Peppery Corn Sauce

4 servings

4 1- to 1¼-inch-thick pork loin chops, about 2¼ pounds total
Salt and freshly ground pepper

1 17-ounce can cream-style corn
¼ cup chopped red bell pepper

¼ cup chopped green bell pepper
2 tablespoons vinegar
1 tablespoon soy sauce
1½ teaspoons firmly packed brown sugar

Place heavy large skillet over high heat 1½ minutes. Pat chops dry with paper towels. Add chops to hot skillet and sear 3 to 4 minutes per side. Season with salt and pepper. Arrange in single layer in 2-quart baking dish.

Preheat oven to 350°F. Combine remaining ingredients in medium bowl and mix thoroughly. Spoon sauce over chops. Cover and bake until sauce is bubbly and chops are cooked through, about 45 minutes. Serve hot.

Saturday Night Jambalaya

A perfect casual party entrée or accompaniment to meat and fried fish. Have the butcher cut ribs into strips.

8 servings

8 ounces beef round steak, trimmed and cut into 1-inch cubes
Salt and freshly ground pepper
½ cup bacon drippings
1 rack pork spareribs (about 2½ pounds), cut into 1-inch strips
2 medium onions, chopped
6 green onions, chopped

¼ cup minced fresh parsley
3 medium garlic cloves, minced
2 cups uncooked pecan rice*
3 cups (or more) chicken stock
1 pound andouille sausage,** cut into chunks
2 teaspoons salt
¾ teaspoon cayenne pepper

Season beef with salt and pepper. Melt bacon drippings in heavy very large saucepan over medium-high heat until very hot. Pat beef dry. Separate ribs and pat dry. Add beef and ribs to pan in batches and brown well. Remove and set aside. Add onions, parsley and garlic to pan and stir until golden. Pour in 3 cups stock. Add beef, ribs, sausage, salt and cayenne and bring to boil, stirring constantly. Reduce heat to low, cover tightly and cook 45 minutes. Check rice for tenderness; if mixture appears dry but rice is not yet tender, add more stock and continue cooking. Turn mixture into bowl and fluff with fork. Serve immediately.

*Available at specialty food stores. Long-grain white rice can be substituted.
**A thick, cooked French pork sausage. If not available, substitute smoked sausage.

Red Beans and Rice with Smoked Sausage

A traditional New Orleans favorite.

4 servings

1 pound dried red beans, rinsed and sorted

1½ pounds smoked sausage, cut into chunks
8 ounces smoked ham shanks
1 large onion, chopped
1 green bell pepper, seeded, deveined and chopped
1 celery stalk, chopped

1 garlic clove, finely chopped
1 teaspoon dried thyme, crumbled
1 teaspoon freshly ground pepper
½ teaspoon ground sage
1 bay leaf
Pinch of cayenne pepper or to taste
Salt
Freshly cooked rice

Place beans in Dutch oven and cover generously with water. Let soak 30 minutes.

Add all remaining ingredients to beans except salt and rice. Bring to boil over medium-high heat. Reduce heat to medium-low, cover and simmer until beans are tender, adding more water if necessary, about 2½ hours. Add salt to taste. Discard ham bones. Remove about 3 tablespoons beans from mixture and mash to paste. Return to Dutch oven and stir through. Simmer 15 more minutes. Serve hot over rice.

Sautéed Country Ham

Accompany with boiled potatoes and crisply cooked green beans.

6 servings

3 tablespoons unsalted butter
6 to 8 slices country ham
   (about ⅛ inch thick)
¼ cup dry white wine

Reserved pan juices from ham
Sugar (optional)
Vinegar (optional)

Melt butter in large nonaluminum skillet over medium-high heat. Add ham in batches and sear on both sides. Transfer to ovenproof platter and keep warm in low oven. Add wine and pan juices to skillet and reduce over high heat until rich in flavor. If sauce is too salty (this will depend upon type of ham used), add a bit of sugar and vinegar for a sweet-sour effect. Pour sauce over ham slices and serve immediately.

Slivered Country Ham with Finger Biscuits

Accompany with crocks of coarse mustard, a smooth herbed mustard, pickled watermelon rind and Jerusalem artichoke or green tomato relish to cut the rich saltiness of the ham.

12 to 16 buffet servings

1 11- to 14-pound country ham
   (see note)

1 bottle (750 ml) tawny Port
2 to 3 cups dry white wine
1 garlic clove, lightly crushed

Beef or chicken stock as needed

Finger Biscuits*
Parsley sprigs (optional garnish)

Scrub ham with soap and warm water; rinse thoroughly. Place ham in large container and cover with cold water. Set in cool place and soak for 24 hours. Change water and soak another 24 hours.

Preheat oven to 350°F. Remove ham from soaking liquid and set skin side down in deep roasting pan. Add Port, white wine and garlic. Cover tightly with foil and bake 2 hours.

Remove ham from pan and let cool briefly. Trim away skin (save for flavoring stews and soups) and fat, leaving thin, even layer. Return ham to pan fat side up. Bake uncovered another 1½ to 2 hours, basting often with pan juices (add stock if pan juices are skimpy), or until meat thermometer inserted in thickest part of ham registers 155°F. Remove from oven and let cool to room temperature. Transfer to platter, slice and serve, or refrigerate 1 to 2 days.

If refrigerating, bring ham to room temperature before slicing and serving. To carve, start at shank end by cutting away a small wedge-shaped piece. Set aside. Now shave small, paper-thin slices, working toward large end of ham. Place partially carved ham on serving platter and surround with warm ham-filled finger biscuits. Accompany with relishes and crocks of mustards. Carve more ham as needed. If desired, garnish platter with fresh parsley.

Leftover ham will keep in refrigerator for 4 to 5 days, or in freezer for several months. Before freezing, trim meat from bone and freeze separately.

*Finger Biscuits

12 servings

2 cups unbleached all purpose flour
2 cups cake flour (do not use self-rising)
2 tablespoons plus 2 teaspoons baking powder

1 teaspoon salt
½ cup (1 stick) well-chilled unsalted butter, cut into small pieces
1¼ to 1½ cups chilled milk

Preheat oven to 425°F. Grease baking sheet. Combine dry ingredients in deep bowl. Using pastry blender, cut in butter until mixture resembles coarse meal. Add milk and toss gently with fork. *Do not overmix; use only enough milk to make dough moist but not wet. (Can be prepared 1 day ahead, wrapped and refrigerated overnight.)* Turn dough out onto floured surface and gently knead only 2 or 3 times. Roll or pat into ½-inch-thick rectangle. Cut into 1-inch squares. Transfer to prepared sheet, spacing about ⅛ inch apart. Bake until puffed and golden, 10 to 15 minutes.

If baking biscuits ahead, let cool, then slit each on 3 sides. Immediately transfer to airtight plastic bags and freeze (they dry out quickly). Defrost in refrigerator the day before serving. Shortly before serving, warm in 350°F oven about 8 minutes or until biscuits are heated through.

Baked Smoked Ham with Apple Cider-Mustard Sauce

Arrange ham on a bed of fresh watercress and surround with tiny poached crabapples. Banana squash flavored with ginger and a casserole of braised fennel are savory accompaniments.

8 to 10 servings

1 8- to 10-pound smoked ham (with bone)

1 cup Spicy Molasses Mustard*
1 cup firmly packed brown sugar
⅓ cup whole mustard seeds
30 to 40 whole cloves

2 cups hard cider
2 tablespoons cider vinegar
2 tablespoons apple jelly
2 tablespoons Spicy Molasses Mustard

Combine ham in large stockpot with enough water to cover. Place over medium-high heat and bring to boil. Reduce heat to low and simmer 2 hours. Let ham cool in liquid.

Preheat oven to 450°F. Strip rind from ham, leaving ½ inch of fat. Score 1-inch crisscross rows into ham using tip of sharp knife. Coat ham with 1 cup mustard. Pat brown sugar over entire surface. Sprinkle with mustard seeds and stud with whole cloves. Transfer to large roasting pan. Bake uncovered until crust is golden brown, about 30 to 40 minutes. Transfer ham to heated platter. Let stand 20 minutes.

Meanwhile, discard any burned sugar from roasting pan. Add cider to pan, place over medium heat and cook until syrupy and reduced to 1½ cups. Increase heat to high, add vinegar and cook, stirring constantly, 1 minute. Add apple jelly and remaining mustard and cook until bubbly and slightly thickened. Strain into sauceboat. Carve ham into ½-inch slices and serve with sauce.

*Spicy Molasses Mustard

This hot mustard goes well with grilled sausages and cold meats.

Makes about 1 cup

1 cup dry mustard
6 tablespoons water or beer
6 tablespoons molasses
6 tablespoons cider vinegar

½ teaspoon *each* ground allspice, cinnamon, salt and freshly ground pepper
¼ teaspoon ground cloves

Combine mustard and water or beer in stainless steel bowl and whisk until well blended. Let stand 15 minutes. Add remaining ingredients and blend well. Transfer to jar with tight-fitting lid. Store in cool, dark place.

Aileen's Ham Loaf

8 to 10 servings

2 tablespoons (¼ stick) butter
1 small onion, minced
8 large mushrooms, finely chopped

2 pounds finely ground cooked
   lean ham (about 6 cups)

1 cup shredded Swiss cheese
1 egg, beaten
¼ cup chicken stock, preferably
   homemade
   Horseradish Sauce*

Oil 10 × 5 × 3-inch loaf pan. Melt butter in medium saucepan over medium heat. Add onion and sauté until translucent. Add mushrooms and sauté until liquid has evaporated. Let cool.

Preheat oven to 325°F. Combine ham, cheese, egg, chicken stock and cooled mushroom mixture in large bowl, blending lightly. Turn into prepared pan, pressing gently. Bake until lightly browned, about 35 to 40 minutes. Let cool about 5 minutes. Invert onto serving platter. Serve loaf hot, warm or chilled. Accompany with sauce.

*Horseradish Sauce

½ cup whipping cream, whipped
3 tablespoons horseradish
   (preferably freshly ground)
1 tablespoon cider vinegar

1 teaspoon sugar
¼ teaspoon salt
   Pinch of freshly ground pepper

Mix all ingredients in medium bowl. Let stand 30 minutes before serving.

5 ❧ Poultry

Thanks to the recent emphasis on lighter cooking, poultry has been enjoying unprecedented popularity. More and more American cooks are serving meat just two or three times a week, often relying on poultry for equally satisfying meals in between.

Fortunately this trend does not in any way sacrifice flavor or variety. Plenty of cookbooks have been written on poultry alone, and there is room for many more. Chicken, for example, is a spectacularly versatile bird, lending itself by turns to simmering, roasting, deep-frying, sautéing; to pies and casseroles, stews and salads, stuffings and fillings.

The recipes here handsomely reflect this adaptability. Boneless chicken breasts, which cook in practically no time, appear in four distinctive dishes. Mixed chicken parts take a bow in Salt and Pepper Cured Pan-Fried Chicken (page 50), Country Captain (page 53), and Chicken Pot Pie (page 54), while opulent Roast Chicken with Apple Butter Sauce (page 51) calls for a whole roaster.

Rounding out the chapter is a quintet of unusual recipes for game hens, duck and turkey, graced with such all-American ingredients as wild rice, cranberries, pecans and applejack. These imaginative dishes—among them Grilled Duck with Date Sauce (page 56) and Roast Breast of Turkey with Apple, Apricot and Currant Stuffing (page 57)—provide ample proof that poultry's booming popularity is richly deserved.

 *Chicken*

Chicken à la Millcroft

From the historic Millcroft Inn in Milford, Ohio.

4 servings

4 8-ounce boneless whole chicken breasts
½ cup all purpose flour
½ cup (1 stick) butter, clarified
6 tablespoons dry white wine
4 ounces mushrooms, thinly sliced

18 tablespoons (2¼ sticks) unsalted butter

1 small tomato, diced and drained
½ medium-size ripe avocado, diced
Salt and freshly ground pepper

Preheat oven to 400°F. Pat chicken dry. Dredge in flour, shaking off excess. Melt butter in heavy large skillet over medium heat. Brown chicken well on both sides. Transfer to large baking dish. Bake until cooked through, about 10 minutes.

Meanwhile, bring wine to simmer in heavy medium saucepan. Add mushrooms and simmer 1 minute. Reduce heat to very low. Whisk in butter 1 tablespoon at a time, incorporating each piece completely before adding next. Stir in tomato and avocado. Season with salt and pepper.

Arrange chicken on platter. Spoon some of sauce over. Serve immediately, passing remaining sauce separately.

Chicken Paillards with Tricolored Bell Peppers

4 servings

4 6- to 7-ounce boneless chicken breast halves, skinned and trimmed

1 medium-size red bell pepper
1 medium-size green bell pepper
1 medium-size yellow bell pepper*
3 tablespoons olive oil
1 jalapeño pepper, seeds and ribs

discarded, minced
Salt

Freshly ground pepper
¼ cup olive oil
¼ cup all purpose flour
1 tablespoon minced fresh parsley
4 small basil sprigs

Pound each chicken breast between 2 sheets of plastic wrap to thickness of ¼ inch, using flat meat pounder or rolling pin. (*Can be prepared 4 hours ahead. Cover tightly and refrigerate. Bring to room temperature before continuing.*)

Halve bell peppers and discard seeds and ribs. Cut bell peppers into 1½ × ¼-inch strips. Heat 3 tablespoons oil in heavy large skillet over low heat. Add jalapeño pepper and cook until soft, stirring occasionally, about 4 minutes. Add bell peppers and pinch of salt. Cook until tender, stirring frequently, about 15 minutes. Adjust seasoning. (*Can be prepared 1 hour ahead. Let pepper mixture stand at room temperature.*)

Preheat oven to 275°F. Sprinkle chicken with salt and pepper. Heat ¼ cup oil in another heavy large skillet over medium-high heat. Dust chicken with flour, shaking to remove excess. Add to skillet and cook until brown and just tender when pierced with sharp knife, about 2 minutes per side. Arrange in single layer on ovenproof platter and keep warm in oven. Repeat flouring and cooking remaining chicken. Reheat bell peppers over low heat, stirring constantly. Discard any juices accumulated on chicken platter. Spoon bell peppers around chicken using slotted spoon. Sprinkle with parsley. Arrange basil sprig atop each chicken breast. Serve immediately.

*If yellow bell peppers are unavailable, use an additional red bell pepper.

🐦 *Paillards*

"A meal in minutes" might be one definition for paillards. Another would refer to them as thin, boneless slices of meat or poultry that are pounded and then sautéed or grilled to perfect succulence. Often they are topped with a quick-to-make sauce. The meat can be pounded several hours ahead of time, leaving only the sautéing or grilling itself to the last minute.

Though the word itself is French, this selection of recipes for chicken paillards uses all-American ingredients.

- To pound meat for paillards, use a heavy, flat meat pounder, flat-surfaced mallet or rolling pin; do not use a mallet with pointed or jagged edges. Place one piece of chicken or meat between two sheets of plastic wrap or waxed paper. Pound with tapping motions, using even pressure and working from center of meat to outer edge, until chicken is of even thickness. Do not pound too forcefully or meat may tear. Carefully peel off the plastic or paper. (Some butchers will pound the chicken breasts for you.)

- Prepare sauce ingredients before cooking paillards. Cooked chicken will become dry if set aside too long.

- A hot skillet or grill is essential for searing chicken properly. If it sticks, the pan is not hot enough. To check, touch the tip of a chicken breast to skillet or grill; it should sizzle immediately. If not, heat 30 seconds longer and check again. If butter starts to brown, reduce heat slightly.

- Bring chicken to room temperature before cooking to avoid reducing temperature of pan. Do not crowd skillet or grill; this reduces temperature of pan and causes the chicken to stew.

- Turn chicken with a wide spatula or pancake turner to prevent puncturing the meat.

Boneless Breast of Chicken with Country Ham

A chilled Sauvignon Blanc is perfect with this dish.

4 servings

4 large whole chicken breasts, skinned, boned, halved and trimmed
4 ounces cooked country ham, Westphalian ham, or prosciutto, cut into julienne
4 green onions, green part only

1 cup milk
3 eggs
1 cup Seasoned Flour (see recipe for Fillets of Smallmouth Bass with Bacon and Green Onions, page 60)

1 cup fresh breadcrumbs
3 tablespoons butter
¼ cup freshly grated Parmesan cheese

2 cups whipping cream
2¼ cups rich unsalted chicken stock, boiled until reduced to ¼ cup
Salt and freshly ground pepper
1 cup chopped fresh chanterelles or other wild mushrooms

Pound each piece of chicken between 2 sheets of waxed paper to thickness of ¼ to ⅛ inch. Press 2 pieces together to form double thickness. Arrange ¼ of ham and 1 green onion over each, leaving small border at short ends. Fold in short ends. With long edge toward you, roll up as for jelly roll.

Whisk milk and eggs in bowl. Dredge chicken in seasoned flour, shaking off excess. Dip in milk mixture, allowing excess to drip back into bowl. Coat thoroughly with breadcrumbs, pressing gently. Arrange chicken on rack in baking pan. Refrigerate until crumbs are set, about 15 minutes.

Preheat oven to 350°F. Melt butter in heavy large skillet over medium-high heat. Add chicken and cook until crumbs brown well on all sides. Return chicken to rack in pan. Bake until almost tender, 10 to 15 minutes. Sprinkle with Parmesan. Continue baking until tender, about 5 minutes.

Meanwhile, boil cream until reduced by half. Stir in reduced stock and boil until mixture is thickened to saucelike consistency. Season generously with salt and freshly ground pepper. Add chanterelles and heat through.

Cut chicken diagonally into thin slices. Spoon sauce onto heated plates. Arrange slices in circle atop sauce. Serve chicken immediately.

Maple Chicken Breasts

4 servings

2 tablespoons all purpose flour
1/8 teaspoon salt
4 whole chicken breasts, boned and halved
1/4 cup (1/2 stick) butter

6 large mushrooms, sliced
1 cup diced onion
1/4 cup maple syrup
Freshly cooked rice

Preheat oven to 350°F. Combine flour and salt in shallow dish. Dredge chicken in flour, shaking off excess. Melt butter in heavy large skillet over medium-low heat. Add mushrooms and sauté until tender, about 4 minutes. Remove with slotted spoon; keep warm. Increase heat to medium-high. Add chicken and onion and cook until chicken is browned and onion is tender, turning chicken once, about 4 minutes per side. Transfer to 1 1/2-quart baking dish. Top with mushrooms. Pour maple syrup evenly over mushrooms. Bake until heated through, about 30 minutes. Serve immediately over rice.

Salt and Pepper Cured Pan-Fried Chicken

4 servings

1 3-pound chicken, cut into 8 pieces, trimmed
1/4 cup coarsely cracked peppercorns
2 cups coarse salt

3 cups (about) milk

1 cup all purpose flour
1 teaspoon cornmeal

1 1/2 cups (about) peanut oil

Arrange chicken in single layer in shallow dish. Sprinkle with pepper, turning pieces to coat completely. Pack salt over and around chicken. Let stand at room temperature 2 1/2 hours.

Rinse chicken in cold water; dry thoroughly. Clean dish; add chicken. Pour in milk to cover. Chill 2 hours.

Drain chicken. Combine flour and cornmeal in another shallow dish. Coat chicken with mixture, shaking off excess (make sure skin is stretched around each piece). Arrange chicken in single layer on rack. Refrigerate uncovered for at least 4 hours.

Heat 1/2 to 3/4 inch oil in cast-iron or other heavy large skillet to 375°F. Add dark meat pieces (they should be only half submerged). Fry 4 minutes, then turn and fry second side 4 minutes. Add white meat and continue frying until chicken is golden brown and cooked through, turning pieces 3 to 4 times, 15 to 20 minutes. Drain on paper towels for 5 minutes and serve.

Roast Chicken with Apple Butter Sauce

A specialty at The Green-brier, the venerable resort in White Sulphur Springs, West Virginia.

3 to 4 servings

1 3-pound chicken
  Salt and freshly ground pepper
2 tablespoons (¼ stick) butter
1 cup diced onion
1 cup diced leek
1 cup diced carrot
1 cup diced celery
1 bay leaf
1 fresh thyme sprig or
  ½ teaspoon dried, crumbled

1 fresh rosemary sprig or
  ½ teaspoon dried, crumbled

½ cup applejack or Calvados
½ cup dry white wine
2 cups Chicken Velouté*
1 cup whipping cream
½ cup apple butter

Preheat oven to 375°F. Sprinkle inside of chicken with salt and pepper. Truss chicken; pat dry. Melt butter in heavy roasting pan over medium heat. Add onion, leek, carrot and celery and cook until softened, stirring frequently, about 15 minutes. Set chicken atop vegetables. Transfer to oven and roast 35 minutes. Add bay leaf, thyme and rosemary and continue roasting until drumsticks move easily in sockets and juices run clear when thighs are pierced, 10 minutes.

Remove chicken from pan and keep warm. Degrease pan juices. Pour apple-jack into corner of pan and warm over medium-high heat. Ignite, shaking pan gently until flames subside. Add wine and cook 3 minutes. Blend in velouté, cream and apple butter and cook 3 minutes. Strain sauce into heavy medium saucepan. Season with salt and pepper. Rewarm over low heat. Carve chicken and arrange on platter. Spoon some of sauce over and serve. Pass remaining sauce separately.

*Chicken Velouté

Makes 2 cups

¼ cup (½ stick) butter
1½ teaspoons minced shallot
1 small bay leaf
½ cup all purpose flour

1½ cups rich chicken stock,
  preferably homemade
¼ cup dry white wine
  Salt and freshly ground pepper

Melt butter in heavy medium saucepan over medium heat. Add shallot and bay leaf and stir until shallot is translucent, about 5 minutes. Reduce heat to medium-low, add flour and whisk 3 minutes. Whisk in stock and wine. Simmer 30 minutes, stirring occasionally. Season with salt and pepper. Strain sauce. Use immediately, or cool completely and refrigerate. Bring to room temperature before using.

Green Chili-Chicken Salad

6 servings

Tarragon Vinaigrette
¼ cup tarragon vinegar
¼ cup vegetable oil
2½ teaspoons lemon pepper

2½ cups diced cooked chicken
½ teaspoon lemon pepper
1 1-pound head iceberg
  lettuce, cored
1 cup chopped tomatoes

½ cup grated longhorn cheese
  (about 2 ounces)
½ cup grated Monterey Jack cheese
  (about 2 ounces)
½ cup canned diced green chilies
½ cup toasted pine nuts

For vinaigrette: Combine vinegar, oil and 2½ teaspoons lemon pepper in small bowl and whisk thoroughly.

Toss chicken with ½ teaspoon lemon pepper in medium bowl. Line large serving bowl with 4 or 5 lettuce leaves. Chop remaining lettuce into bite-size pieces. Transfer to serving bowl. Add remaining ingredients and toss lightly. Pour dressing over and toss again. Refrigerate salad for 10 to 15 minutes before serving.

Avocado Rellenos

8 servings

6 poblano or Anaheim chilies

4 medium-size ripe but firm avocados
2 lemons, halved
Salt
1 pound shredded cooked chicken

2 cups fine dry breadcrumbs
¼ cup freshly grated Parmesan cheese

2 cups Old Texas Tomato Sauce*
1½ cups beef stock

⅔ cup tomato sauce
¼ teaspoon dried oregano, crumbled
Freshly ground pepper

Vegetable oil (for deep frying)
8 eggs, separated
6 tablespoons cake flour
½ teaspoon salt

Chopped green onion
Red chile salsa (optional)

Char chilies over gas flame or under broiler, turning until skins blacken. Steam in plastic bag 10 minutes. Remove skin, seeds and cores (wear rubber gloves or oil hands to prevent burning). Rinse, pat dry and chop.

Peel and halve avocados. Scoop out small circular section (in one piece) from center of each half to widen and deepen cavity and reserve. Squeeze lemon juice over each half. Sprinkle lightly with salt. Combine chicken and chilies and pack 1½ tablespoons filling into each cavity. Set reserved section on top and press down to seal edges.

Combine breadcrumbs and cheese. Coat each avocado half with thin layer, shaking off excess.

Bring Old Texas Tomato Sauce, beef stock, tomato sauce, oregano, salt and pepper to boil in heavy medium saucepan. Keep sauce warm over low heat.

Heat 3½ to 4 inches of oil in deep fryer or heavy deep skillet to 375°F. Beat yolks and flour in mixer bowl until thick enough for ribbon to form when beaters are lifted. Beat whites and salt in another bowl until stiff but not dry. Gently fold ¼ of whites into yolk mixture, then fold yolk mixture back into remaining whites.

Shape 2 heaping tablespoons batter into oval and drop into oil. Immediately slide broad metal spatula under. Quickly set avocado half on top of batter. Cover exposed surface with more batter. Spoon hot oil over to seal. Fry until all sides are brown, turning frequently, about 2½ minutes total. Drain on paper towels. Repeat with remaining avocado halves.

Set relleno on plate. Spoon some sauce over. Sprinkle with chopped green onion. Pass salsa separately if desired.

*Old Texas Tomato Sauce

Also great over tamales or pasta.

Makes 1 quart

5 large tomatoes (do not core) or one 28-ounce can Italian plum tomatoes, drained
¼ cup vegetable or olive oil
1 medium onion, minced
¾ cup beef stock
½ cup red wine vinegar

3 tablespoons tomato paste
6 fresh basil leaves *or* 5 cilantro sprigs
1 teaspoon salt
Freshly ground pepper
¾ cup loosely packed fresh parsley or cilantro leaves, minced

Preheat broiler. Broil fresh tomatoes 4 inches from heat source until skin is softened, turning occasionally. Puree in blender until smooth. (If using canned plum tomatoes, first break up with fork, then puree.)

Heat oil in heavy medium skillet over medium-high heat. Add onion and stir 4 minutes. Blend in tomato puree, stock, vinegar, tomato paste, basil, salt and pepper and cook until reduced and thickened to saucelike consistency, stirring occasionally, about 10 minutes. Puree in blender until smooth. Stir in parsley. Serve sauce warm or at room temperature.

Country Captain Chicken

Country Captain is a traditional favorite with many variations. This rendition is a light sauté, with a sauce prepared separately.

2 to 4 servings

Curry Mixture
- 4 bay leaves, coarsely crumbled
- 2 tablespoons cumin seeds
- 2 tablespoons coriander seeds
- 1 cinnamon stick, broken into pieces
- 1 tablespoon black peppercorns
- 1 teaspoon fennel seeds
- 1 teaspoon turmeric
- ½ teaspoon whole allspice

- 1 3- to 3½-pound chicken

  Salt and freshly ground pepper
- 3 tablespoons peanut oil

- ¼ cup dry white wine
- ¾ cup (or more) chicken stock, preferably homemade

- 2 medium-size red bell peppers, cut into matchstick julienne
- 2 medium-size green bell peppers, cut into matchstick julienne
- 2 medium tomatoes, peeled, seeded and diced
- 1 medium onion, halved and very thinly sliced
- 3 medium-size green onions, thinly sliced
- 2 tablespoons chutney

  Freshly cooked white or brown rice
  Toasted slivered almonds
  Dried currants

For curry mixture: Grind all spices to powder in small hand or electric grinder or in mortar with pestle.

Remove wings and back from chicken and reserve for another use. Cut remaining chicken into 2 legs, 2 thighs and 2 half breasts. Trim excess skin and fat from chicken.

Preheat oven to 400°F. Pat chicken dry. Season with salt and pepper. Heat oil in heavy large skillet over medium-high heat. Add chicken in single layer skin side down and brown lightly, about 5 minutes. Turn and brown other side. Transfer chicken to shallow baking dish using slotted spoon. Bake until just cooked through, 10 to 15 minutes. Bone breast pieces.

Pour off excess fat from skillet. Set over low heat. Stir in 1 teaspoon curry mixture (reserve remainder for another use). Add wine, scraping up browned bits. Boil until wine is reduced by half. Add ¾ cup stock and reduce by half. Stir in red and green bell peppers, tomatoes and onion. Reduce heat, cover and simmer until peppers are tender, about 5 minutes. Adjust sauce consistency, if necessary, by boiling if too thin or adding 2 to 3 tablespoons more stock if too thick. Blend in half of green onion and 2 tablespoons chutney. Mix chicken into sauce. Simmer until heated through.

Mound rice on platter. Top with chicken. Spoon sauce over. Garnish with remaining green onion. Sprinkle with nuts and currants and serve.

Chicken Pot Pie

A famous Pennsylvania Dutch specialty. This dish is not actually a pie, but a chicken soup-stew with homemade noodles.

6 to 8 servings

1 4- to 5-pound roasting or stewing chicken, cut into pieces
3 quarts (or more) water
3 celery stalks (with leaves), chopped
1 small onion, coarsely chopped
6 to 8 peppercorns
1 tablespoon salt

3 medium boiling potatoes, peeled and cut into 1/2- to 3/4-inch slices

2 to 3 medium leeks (white part only), washed and thinly sliced
3/4 cup sliced celery
3 tablespoons minced fresh parsley
1/4 teaspoon crushed saffron threads or ground saffron
Pot Pie Noodle Squares*
Salt and freshly ground pepper

Combine chicken in large saucepan with enough water to cover and bring to boil, skimming foam from surface as it accumulates. Reduce heat and add chopped celery, onion, peppercorns and salt. Simmer until chicken is tender, about 30 to 45 minutes. Remove chicken from broth using slotted spoon and set aside until cool enough to handle. Discard skin and bones; cut meat into 1-inch pieces.

Strain broth. Measure 2 quarts into large saucepan and bring to boil. Add potato, leek, sliced celery, parsley and saffron and cook over medium-high heat 5 minutes. Carefully stir in noodle squares and continue cooking until noodles are tender, about 12 to 15 minutes. Add chicken and heat through. Season with salt and pepper to taste. Ladle into bowls and serve.

*Pot Pie Noodle Squares

Makes about 24 2-inch squares

1 1/2 cups (or more) all purpose flour
3/4 teaspoon baking powder
1/2 teaspoon salt

2 eggs
1 teaspoon cold water

Combine 1 1/2 cups flour, baking powder and salt in large mixing bowl. Beat eggs with water in small bowl and blend into dry ingredients, mixing thoroughly and adding more flour if necessary (dough should be stiff). Turn dough out onto lightly floured surface and roll to thickness of 1/16 inch (or as thin as possible). Cut into 2-inch squares with pinking shears or sharp knife.

❦ *Game Hens, Duck and Turkey*

Wild Rice-Stuffed Game Hens with Caraway Cream Sauce

Perfect for entertaining: The hens can be prepared and stuffed before the guests arrive, then roasted while cocktails are served.

4 servings

2 tablespoons (1/4 stick) butter
8 ounces mushrooms, sliced
4 medium-size green onions, chopped
2 small pork sausage patties (3 ounces total), crumbled
4 game hens, giblets chopped
1 3/4 cups chicken stock
1 cup wild rice
3/4 cup dry white wine
1/4 cup minced fresh parsley

1 teaspoon dried basil, crumbled
Salt and freshly ground pepper

1/4 cup (1/2 stick) butter, melted
Chicken stock (if necessary)

Sauce
1/4 cup (1/2 stick) butter
3 tablespoons all purpose flour
1 teaspoon caraway seeds
3/4 cup whipping cream
1/2 cup chicken stock

Melt 2 tablespoons butter in large saucepan over medium-low heat. Sauté mushrooms and green onions until onions are soft, about 10 minutes. Add sausage and sauté until cooked through, 3 to 4 minutes. Remove mushroom mixture with slotted spoon and set aside. Reduce heat to low and add chopped giblets, 1¾ cups stock, wild rice, wine, parsley and basil. Season with salt and pepper. Cook stuffing until all liquid is absorbed, about 40 minutes.

Preheat oven to 375°F. Remove stuffing from heat and stir in half of mushroom mixture; set remainder aside. Fill hens with stuffing. Transfer to roasting pan. Brush each generously with melted butter. Roast 1¼ hours, basting frequently with melted butter. Remove hens from pan and keep warm. Degrease pan juices and pour into measuring cup. Add stock, if needed, to equal 1 cup. Reserve.

For sauce: Melt ¼ cup butter in heavy small saucepan over low heat. Combine flour and caraway in small bowl. Whisk into butter. Cook, whisking constantly, until roux is frothy and smooth, about 3 minutes. Whisk in whipping cream and ½ cup chicken stock. Add 1 cup pan juices and remaining mushroom mixture. Cook until smooth, about 4 minutes. Serve hens immediately with sauce.

Duck Breasts with Cranberries

An ideal holiday-season entrée. The chestnut soufflé is a rich accompaniment.

4 servings

¼ cup sugar
¼ cup water
½ cup red wine vinegar

2 whole duck breasts, boned and halved
Coarse salt
Freshly ground pepper
2 cups rich veal stock, preferably homemade

1½ cups cranberries
½ cup dry red wine

¼ cup cranberry liqueur
2 tablespoons (¼ stick) unsalted butter
1 bunch watercress
Chestnut Soufflé*

Heat sugar and water in heavy small saucepan over low heat until sugar dissolves, swirling pan occasionally. Increase heat and boil until caramelized to rich brown. Swirl pan, if necessary, until mixture is saucelike consistency. Remove from heat and pour in vinegar (be careful; mixture will bubble).

Pat duck dry. Using sharp knife, score skin in crisscross pattern. Rub salt and pepper into skin. Heat heavy large skillet over medium-high heat until very hot. Add duck skin side down and cook until skin is brown and meat is medium-rare, pouring off fat from pan, about 10 minutes. Turn duck over and quickly sear second side, about 2 minutes. Remove duck from skillet. Pour off fat from skillet. Stir caramel into skillet, scraping up browned bits. Add stock, cranberries and red wine and boil until sauce is reduced by half, 10 to 15 minutes.

Preheat broiler. Broil duck until crisp. Cut lengthwise into thin slices. Arrange in fan shape on plate. Remove sauce from heat. Blend in liqueur and butter. Taste and adjust seasoning. Spoon sauce over duck. Garnish with watercress. Serve with chestnut soufflé.

*Chestnut Soufflé

4 servings

1 tablespoon butter
1 tablespoon all purpose flour
½ cup milk
3 eggs, separated, room temperature
½ cup drained canned chestnuts, pureed

Salt and freshly ground white pepper
Pinch of cream of tartar
4 whole canned chestnuts

Preheat oven to 375°F. Butter four 5- to 6-ounce molds. Dust with flour, shaking out excess. Melt 1 tablespoon butter in heavy medium saucepan over medium-low heat. Add 1 tablespoon flour and stir 3 minutes. Blend in milk. Increase heat and bring to boil. Stir until thick, about 5 minutes. Remove from heat. Add yolks and chestnut puree and stir until smooth. Season with salt and pepper. Beat whites with cream of tartar until stiff but not dry. Gently fold ¼ of whites into chestnut mixture to loosen, then fold in remaining whites. Divide mixture among prepared molds. Set 1 chestnut in center of each. Bake soufflés until puffed, about 25 minutes. Run knife around edge. Unmold each soufflé onto plate and serve.

Grilled Duck with Date Sauce

Merlot is a good wine to accompany this rich entrée. Remaining date puree can be used as an accompaniment to grilled pork or chicken.

4 servings

7 tablespoons Port
¼ cup Duck Stock*
8 dates, pitted

1 cup firmly packed light brown sugar
½ cup dark molasses
½ cup honey
½ cup maple syrup
¾ cup water

10 tablespoons (1¼ sticks) unsalted butter

4 whole duck breasts, skinned, boned and halved

¼ cup raspberry vinegar
2 tablespoons minced shallots

2 cups whipping cream
Salt

Combine 4 tablespoons Port and stock in heavy medium saucepan. Add dates. Let stand 3 hours at room temperature or refrigerate overnight.

Combine brown sugar, molasses, honey, syrup, ¼ cup water, remaining 3 tablespoons Port and 2 tablespoons butter in heavy medium saucepan over low heat and stir until melted. Cool marinade to room temperature.

Pour marinade into pan. Add duck and marinate 1 hour, turning once.

Add ¼ cup water, vinegar, shallots and remaining 8 tablespoons butter to date mixture. Simmer until dates are tender and almost all liquid is absorbed, stirring occasionally, about 20 minutes. Transfer to processor. Add ¼ cup water and puree until smooth.

Boil cream until reduced by half. Stir in ¼ cup date puree. Keep warm.

Prepare barbecue grill (or preheat broiler). Remove duck from marinade; pat dry. Grill duck about 4 inches from heat source for 2½ minutes. Turn and grill on second side 1½ minutes (for rare). Cut duck into thin diagonal slices. Spoon sauce onto plates. Overlap duck slices atop sauce and serve.

*Duck Stock

Makes about 4 cups

Bones from 4 ducks, chopped

2 large carrots, chopped
2 celery stalks (with leaves), chopped
2 large onions, quartered
1 large tomato, quartered
1 large leek, sliced

½ cup dry red wine
½ cup red wine vinegar
2 tablespoons cracked black pepper
2 garlic cloves, crushed
Bouquet garni (thyme, bay leaf, parsley stems)

Preheat oven to 425°F. Arrange bones in roasting pan. Roast until browned, turning occasionally, about 45 minutes.

Pour off fat from pan. Add carrots, celery, onions, tomato and leek. Roast until browned, about 20 minutes.

Country Captain Chicken

True Texas Chili

*Clockwise from top right:
Chocolate Coconut Flan;
Avocado Rellenos with Old
Texas Tomato Sauce; Savory
Cheese and Chili Churros*

Clockwise from top: Sweet Potato Pecan Torte with Maple Cream; Mincemeat Cornucopias in Apple Brandy Sauce; Peter's Frozen Pumpkin Mousse in Lace Shells

Boardinghouse Meat Pie

Transfer bones and vegetables to stockpot. Pour off fat from roasting pan. Stir wine and vinegar into roasting pan and cook over high heat, scraping up browned bits. Pour mixture into stockpot. Add pepper, garlic and bouquet garni. Pour in enough cold water to cover ingredients. Bring to boil. Reduce heat and simmer 4 hours, skimming foam from surface.

Strain stock. Cool completely. Cover and refrigerate overnight.

Discard fat from surface of stock. Boil stock until reduced by half, skimming foam from surface. Let cool. Store in airtight container. (*Can be prepared 3 days ahead and refrigerated.*)

Turkey Salad with Pecans and Cranberries

4 to 6 servings

½ cup fresh parsley leaves
¼ cup fresh orange juice
1 egg yolk
1½ tablespoons cider vinegar
1 tablespoon sugar
1½ teaspoons Dijon mustard
½ teaspoon salt
6 tablespoons safflower oil

1½ cups cranberries
4 cups cooked turkey meat, cut into ¾-inch cubes
3 large celery stalks with leaves, thickly sliced
1¼ cups pecans, coarsely chopped
Lettuce leaves

Mince parsley in food processor fitted with steel knife. Add orange juice, yolk, vinegar, sugar, mustard and salt to work bowl and blend until smooth. With machine running, pour oil through feed tube in slow stream. Carefully remove steel knife and insert medium slicer.

Place cranberries in feed tube and slice using light pressure. Transfer berry mixture to large bowl. Mix in turkey and celery. Refrigerate at least 1 hour. (*Can be prepared 1 day ahead.*) Mix in pecans. Arrange lettuce leaves on chilled plates. Top with salad and serve.

Roast Breast of Turkey with Apple, Apricot and Currant Stuffing

12 to 14 servings

7 tablespoons diced dried apricots
3½ tablespoons dried currants
6 tablespoons (¾ stick) unsalted butter, room temperature
½ medium onion, chopped
6 tablespoons slivered almonds
2 medium-size tart green apples, peeled, cored and diced
2¼ cups dry breadcrumbs
½ teaspoon salt
¼ teaspoon dried sage, crumbled
3 to 4 tablespoons chicken stock

1 5- to 5½-pound fresh whole turkey breast, boned and trimmed (do not remove skin)
3 cups apple cider
½ cup applejack
1½ cups crème fraîche
Additional applejack (optional)
Fresh lemon juice (optional)
Fresh sage sprigs

Soak apricots and currants in boiling water to cover until plumped and soft, about 15 minutes. Drain.

Melt 1 tablespoon butter in heavy medium skillet over medium heat. Add onion and cook until slightly softened, stirring occasionally, about 6 minutes. Drain on paper towels.

Melt 1 tablespoon butter in same skillet over medium heat. Add almonds and toss until golden brown, 2 to 3 minutes. Drain on paper towels.

Melt 2 tablespoons butter in same skillet over medium heat. Add apples and cook until slightly softened, tossing occasionally, about 5 minutes. Drain apples on paper towels.

Combine apricots, currants, onion, almonds, apples, breadcrumbs, salt and dried sage. Blend in 3 tablespoons chicken stock. If stuffing is too dry, add 1 more tablespoon stock. Adjust seasoning with salt. Cool completely. (*Can be prepared 1 day ahead and refrigerated.*)

To butterfly turkey, lay meat skin side down in front of you (shape should resemble heart). Starting at center, hold knife parallel to meat with blade pointed to left and make lengthwise cut through meat on left side; do not cut to edge. Open flap. Turn meat and repeat on right side. Spread meat out flat. Cover with waxed paper. Gently pound to thickness of ½ to ¾ inch. Season generously with salt. Spread with stuffing, leaving ½-inch border. Starting with long edge, roll meat into 16 × 3-inch cylinder. Tie at 1- to 2-inch intervals with kitchen twine. Secure ends with toothpicks.

Preheat oven to 350°F. Mix cider and applejack. Rub turkey with remaining 2 tablespoons butter. Set on rack in roasting pan. Roast until skin is browned and juices run clear when meat is pierced with knife, basting every 15 minutes with ½ cup cider mixture, about 1 hour. Let stand 15 minutes.

Meanwhile, degrease basting liquid. Pour into measuring cup. Add enough remaining cider mixture to equal 1½ cups liquid total. Stir back into roasting pan over high heat, scraping up browned bits. Add crème fraîche and boil until sauce thickens. Strain sauce. Season with salt. If sauce is too sweet, add applejack and lemon juice to taste. Discard twine and toothpicks from turkey. Cut turkey into ½- to ¾-inch slices. Arrange on platter. Garnish with sage. Pass sauce separately.

6 🍎 Seafood

With our 12,000-plus miles of coastline—not to mention innumerable rivers and lakes—it is no wonder that American cooks have developed an impressive repertoire of fish and shellfish dishes. Naturally, they reflect regional culinary styles as well as the local catch. The Louisiana bayous boast spicy Blackened Redfish (page 61) and Acadian Peppered Shrimp (page 69); New England contributes Massachusetts Fish Stew (page 72) and Tollgate Hill Shellfish Pie (page 70); middle-Atlantic epicures have devised Scallops Chesapeake and Beachway Oyster Fritters (both on page 68). Gumbos and crab cakes are trademark dishes of the Deep South, while salmon is equally representative of the Pacific Northwest.

Like poultry, seafood is becoming ever more popular as we moderate our meat consumption. There is just one essential rule to remember for any kind of fish or shellfish: *don't overcook*. In the past, all too many recipes called for cooking fish until it flakes—which is virtually guaranteed to make it tough, dry and tasteless. Fish and scallops should be cooked until opaque; clams and mussels, until they open; shrimp, until they turn pink—and, with rare exceptions, no longer. As long as other ingredients are prepared in advance, these brief cooking times mean that most seafood dishes, no matter how elegant, are a snap to put together.

Fish

Fried Bass

Freshwater bass, catfish, flounder and red snapper are all good for this dish.

6 to 8 servings

3 to 4 pounds ¾-inch-thick freshwater bass or other firm-fleshed white fish fillets
1 tablespoon salt

3 cups yellow cornmeal
¼ cup all purpose flour

1 tablespoon freshly ground pepper
1 tablespoon cayenne pepper
1½ teaspoons granulated garlic or garlic powder
Vegetable oil (for deep frying)
Lemon and lime wedges

Place bass in large bowl. Cover with water and stir in salt. Marinate in refrigerator for 2 to 3 hours.

Combine cornmeal, flour, pepper, cayenne and garlic in plastic bag. Add fish fillets one at a time and shake to coat. Heat oil in deep fryer or deep saucepan to 350°F. Add fish in batches (do not crowd) and cook until it rises to surface, turning occasionally, about 5 minutes. Transfer fish to paper towels to drain, using slotted spoon. Garnish with lemon and lime and serve.

Fillets of Smallmouth Bass with Bacon and Green Onions

4 servings

8 ounces bacon, sliced

2 pounds fillets of smallmouth bass, crappie, bluegill or trout
2 cups milk
1 cup Seasoned Flour*

1 cup chopped green onions
Lemon wedges
Minced fresh parsley

Cook bacon in heavy large skillet over medium-high heat until crisp. Remove using slotted spoon and drain on paper towels. Pour off all but ½ cup bacon drippings from skillet.

Dip fish fillets in milk. Dredge in seasoned flour, shaking off excess. Rewarm bacon drippings over medium-high heat. Add fish to skillet and cook 2 minutes. Turn fish over. Sprinkle with onions and cook until fish is opaque throughout, about 2 minutes. Transfer to heated plates. Crumble bacon over fish. Garnish with lemon and parsley. Serve immediately.

*Seasoned Flour

Makes about 2¾ cups

2½ cups all purpose flour
1½ tablespoons dried tarragon, crumbled
1 tablespoon salt

2 teaspoons freshly ground pepper
2 teaspoons paprika
½ teaspoon garlic powder
½ teaspoon dry mustard

Blend all ingredients in bowl. Store in airtight container in cool dry place.

Halibut Steaks with Pecans, Celery and Red Bell Pepper

4 servings

2 teaspoons unsalted butter
½ cup pecan halves, halved lengthwise
Salt

¼ cup all purpose flour
4 1-inch-thick halibut steaks (about 1¾ pounds total)
Freshly ground pepper

4 tablespoons (½ stick) unsalted butter
3 tablespoons vegetable oil

2 celery stalks, peeled and cut into 1½ × ¼-inch strips
1 small red bell pepper, cut into 1½ × ¼-inch strips

Melt 2 teaspoons butter in heavy small skillet over medium-low heat. Add pecans and pinch of salt and stir until lightly toasted. Set aside.

Spread flour on large plate. Sprinkle fish on both sides with salt and pepper. Dip in flour to coat both sides, shaking off excess. Arrange fish in single layer on another large plate.

Melt 2 tablespoons butter with oil in heavy large skillet over medium-high heat. Cook fish 4 minutes on first side, reducing heat to medium when browned. Turn fish over, increase heat to medium-high and cook about 4 more minutes (thin skewer inserted in thickest part of fish for 10 seconds will be just hot when touched to inner wrist), reducing heat to medium when browned. Arrange in single layer on heated platter and tent with foil.

Melt remaining 2 tablespoons butter in heavy medium skillet over low heat. Cook celery and bell pepper until just tender, stirring frequently, about 6 minutes. Spoon over fish. Sprinkle with pecans and serve immediately.

Blackened Redfish

For this dish to be a success, the fish must be very cold and the skillet (preferably cast iron) very heavy. And be prepared for a good deal of smoke in the kitchen as the fish cooks.

8 servings

8 10-ounce redfish or red snapper fillets, skinned

2 cups (4 sticks) butter
¼ cup fresh lemon juice

1 tablespoon dried thyme, crumbled
1½ teaspoons cayenne pepper
1 teaspoon salt

Remove any small bones from fish fillets, using tweezers. Keep fish in refrigerator until ready to use.

Melt butter in heavy large skillet over low heat. Stir in lemon juice and seasonings and cook 10 minutes. Pour into wide shallow dish. Cool.

Heat large cast-iron skillet over high heat until bottom begins to form white haze. Pat fish dry. Dip each fillet in butter mixture. Place in skillet; fish will blacken and cook almost immediately. Turn and quickly cook other side (fish will appear burned on outside). Remove from skillet. Repeat with remaining fillets. Cover loosely with foil to keep warm.

Add remaining butter mixture to skillet over high heat. Stir with spoon to scrape up all browned bits and cook until butter is dark brown. Spoon browned butter evenly over fish and serve immediately.

Grilled Salmon Steaks

*For a pretty brunch
presentation, alternate
the salmon and mounds
of scrambled eggs on
one platter.*

6 servings

6 1½-inch-thick salmon steaks,
  skinned
6 thin peppered bacon strips*

  Vegetable oil
6 tablespoons (¾ stick) unsalted
  butter, melted

2½ tablespoons fresh lemon juice
6 lemon wedges

Cut around bone at top of salmon steaks and remove. Trim 1 inch off thin ends
of salmon. Wrap each salmon steak with bacon, securing with toothpick. *(Can
be prepared 6 hours ahead and refrigerated.)*

    Prepare barbecue grill (salmon can also be broiled). Generously coat barbecue
rack with vegetable oil. Combine butter and lemon juice in small bowl. Brush
on one side of salmon. Arrange salmon on grill buttered side down. Cook 5
minutes. Brush top with butter mixture. Turn salmon over and cook until just
opaque, about 5 minutes. Discard toothpicks. Brush salmon with remaining butter. Arrange on heated platter. Garnish with lemon and serve immediately.

*If unavailable, substitute regular bacon sprinkled with crushed black pepper.

Mesquite-Smoked Salmon

*This succulent salmon can
be prepared in a smoker
or barbecue.*

12 servings

1 cup chopped cilantro
½ cup dry white wine
¼ cup soy sauce
¼ cup fresh lemon juice
¼ cup safflower oil
1 5-pound salmon, cleaned, head
  and tail removed

1 quart mesquite chips, soaked in
  water to cover 30 minutes and
  drained

1 medium onion, halved
2 bay leaves
1 cup cilantro leaves and stems
  Cilantro and lemon slices
  Cilantro Sauce*

Combine chopped cilantro, wine, soy sauce and lemon juice in small bowl. Whisk
in oil a drop at a time. Place fish in nonaluminum pan. Pour marinade over.
Refrigerate salmon 4 hours or overnight, turning occasionally.

    Remove fish from marinade and place on rack 30 minutes to drain. Pour
marinade into smoke's water bath.

    Spread mesquite chips on rack of gas or electric smoker.* Add onion and
bay leaves to water bath and fill with water. Fill fish cavity with 1 cup cilantro
leaves and stems. Oil smoker rack and set fish on rack. Cover smoker. Set heat
on high. Smoke salmon until fish is just opaque, about 1 hour. Cool 15 minutes.
Discard skin and gray meat from fish. Set fish on platter. Surround with cilantro
and lemon slices. Serve at room temperature with cilantro sauce.

*To smoke fish in covered barbecue, prepare medium-low coals in barbecue grill. Push coals to sides.
Place marinade, onion and bay leaves in 7 × 11-inch disposable aluminum pan. Place in center of
coals and fill with water. Spread mesquite chips over coals. Oil grill rack. Set fish on rack, cover and
smoke, turning once and cooking until opaque, about 1½ hours.

*Cilantro Sauce

Makes about 3 cups

Mayonnaise
  2 egg yolks, room temperature
  1 egg, room temperature
  2 teaspoons fresh lemon juice
  ½ teaspoon Dijon mustard
  ½ teaspoon salt
  1 cup olive oil
  1 cup safflower oil
  Salt and freshly ground white
  pepper

  ¼ cup chopped green onion
  3 anchovies, chopped
  2 medium garlic cloves
  1 cup chopped cilantro
  1 cup sour cream
  1 tablespoon Cognac
  1 tablespoon grated lemon peel
  2 teaspoons fresh lemon juice

For mayonnaise: Blend yolks, egg, 2 teaspoons lemon juice, mustard and salt in processor. With machine running, slowly pour oils through feed tube. Season with salt and pepper. Refrigerate. *(Can be stored in covered jar 3 days.)*

  With processor running, add green onion, anchovies and garlic through feed tube and mince. Add cilantro and mince using on/off turns. Blend in 1½ cups mayonnaise, sour cream, Cognac, lemon peel and juice. Transfer to bowl. Let sauce stand at room temperature 15 minutes before serving.

Barbecued Swordfish in Herb Marinade

2 servings

  ¼ cup plus 2 tablespoons
    vegetable oil
  ¼ cup chopped onion
  2 tablespoons red wine vinegar
  1 small garlic clove, minced
  1 teaspoon Dijon mustard

  ¼ teaspoon dried basil, crumbled
  ½ bay leaf, crushed
  1 pound swordfish steaks, about
    1 inch thick

Combine first 7 ingredients in shallow dish. Add swordfish, turning several times to coat with marinade. Let stand at least 1 hour, turning occasionally.

  Prepare barbecue. Grill swordfish until opaque, about 5 minutes per side, basting frequently. Serve immediately.

Sole Soufflés with Creole Sauce

The sole mixture can be prepared one hour ahead; fold in egg whites just before baking.

2 servings

  4 ounces fillet of sole
  8 tablespoons water
  1 tablespoon cornstarch
  2 teaspoons fresh lemon juice
  1 teaspoon Dijon mustard
  Salt and freshly ground pepper
  ¼ cup shredded Gruyère or Swiss
    cheese

  2 egg yolks, room temperature,
    beaten to blend
  2 tablespoons minced fresh parsley
  3 egg whites, room temperature
  Creole Sauce*

Preheat oven to 375°F. Lightly butter two 10-ounce soufflé or ovenproof glass dishes. Puree sole with 4 tablespoons water in blender or processor. Dissolve cornstarch in 1 tablespoon water. Heat remaining 3 tablespoons water, lemon juice, mustard, salt and pepper in heavy small saucepan over medium heat. Stir in dissolved cornstarch and whisk until thick. Add to sole puree and blend well. Return to saucepan and stir 1 minute over medium heat. Remove from heat. Mix in 2 tablespoons cheese, yolks and parsley. Using electric mixer, beat whites until stiff but not dry. Fold whites into sole mixture in 2 additions. Spoon into prepared dishes. Sprinkle with remaining cheese. Bake until puffed and golden, 20 to 25 minutes. Serve immediately with Creole sauce.

*Creole Sauce

An all-purpose low-calorie sauce. Also great with hamburgers or pasta.

Makes about ¾ cup

- 2 **tablespoons chicken stock**
- ⅓ **cup thinly sliced red bell pepper**
- ⅓ **cup thinly sliced green bell pepper**
- 2 **tablespoons minced onion**
- 2 **tablespoons minced green onion**
- 2 **tablespoons minced celery**
- ½ **cup chopped fresh or canned tomatoes**

- 2 **tablespoons dry white wine**
- 2 **teaspoons tomato paste**
- ⅛ **teaspoon dried red pepper flakes**
  Salt and freshly ground pepper
- 2 **tablespoons minced fresh parsley**

Heat stock in heavy small skillet over medium heat. Add bell peppers, onions, celery and garlic and cook until softened, stirring frequently, about 5 minutes. Add tomatoes, wine, tomato paste and red pepper flakes and bring to boil. Reduce heat and simmer until sauce thickens, stirring occasionally, about 10 minutes. Season with salt and pepper. Stir in parsley and serve.

Fillet of Sole Florida

4 servings

- 1½ **tablespoons fresh lemon juice, white vinegar or cider vinegar**
- 1 **tablespoon finely chopped shallot**
- ¼ **teaspoon freshly ground white pepper**
- ½ **cup (1 stick) frozen unsalted butter, cut into ½-inch cubes**

- 4 **sole fillets, freshly poached and still warm (see following recipe)**
- 16 **thin slices avocado**
- 8 **grapefruit sections, halved lengthwise**
  Parsley sprigs (garnish)

Combine lemon juice, shallot and pepper in small saucepan over medium heat and cook until liquid is reduced by half. Remove from heat and whisk in butter 2 or 3 pieces at a time, incorporating each piece completely before adding more. After adding several pieces, return pan to very low heat and whisk in remaining butter in same manner. Sauce should be thick and creamy. Remove from heat and continue whisking until pan and sauce cool slightly. Set aside.

   Arrange poached fillets on heated serving platter or individual plates. Top each fillet with alternating slices of avocado and grapefruit. Spoon about 2 tablespoons sauce over each fillet. Garnish with parsley sprigs and serve.

Basic Poached Sole Fillets

4 to 6 servings

- 4 **to 6 medium to large sole fillets**
  Fresh lemon juice
- 2 **tablespoons light vegetable oil (preferably cold-pressed safflower) or unsalted butter**
- 1 **small onion, sliced**

- 1¼ **cups clam juice**
- 1 **tablespoon fresh lemon juice**
- 1 **bay leaf**
- 1 **garlic clove, crushed**
- 6 **peppercorns**

Preheat oven to 350°F. Pat fillets dry. Sprinkle with fresh lemon juice. Roll up fillets, skin side in, and fasten with toothpicks. Set aside.

Heat oil in small flameproof baking dish over medium-high heat. Add onion and sauté 2 minutes. Add clam juice, 1 tablespoon fresh lemon juice, bay leaf, garlic and peppercorns and bring to boil. Add fillets. Cover with sheet of greased waxed paper. Transfer to oven and bake just until fish turns opaque, about 5 to 8 minutes. Immediately transfer fillets to serving platter using long, wide spatula. Strain cooking liquid and reserve for another use.

Trout Hemingway

8 servings

1 cup fresh lemon juice	2 cups (about) all purpose flour
¼ cup water	4 to 5 cups sesame seeds
8 6-ounce fresh lake trout fillets,*	½ cup (1 stick) unsalted butter
1½ to 2 inches thick	Salt

Blend ¾ cup lemon juice and water in large bowl. Dip trout into lemon juice mixture. Dredge in flour, shaking off excess. Dip in lemon juice again. Roll in sesame seeds, pressing gently to cover completely. Melt butter with remaining ¼ cup lemon juice in heavy large skillet. Fry trout until golden brown, about 7 minutes per side. Season with salt and serve.

*If unavailable, use salmon or grouper.

Trout with Roasted Pecans and Creole Meunière Sauce

From Commander's Palace, the renowned New Orleans restaurant.

6 servings

Pecan Butter
½ cup toasted pecans
¼ cup (½ stick) butter, room temperature
1 teaspoon Worcestershire sauce
Juice of ½ medium lemon

Creole Meunière Sauce
2 tablespoons vegetable oil
2 tablespoons all purpose flour
1½ cups fish stock
½ cup (1 stick) butter (room temperature), cut into small pieces
1 to 2 tablespoons Worcestershire sauce
¼ cup chopped fresh parsley
Juice of 1 medium lemon
Salt and freshly ground pepper

Trout
1 cup milk
2 eggs, beaten to blend
1 cup all purpose flour
½ teaspoon garlic powder
½ teaspoon salt
½ teaspoon freshly ground pepper
½ teaspoon cayenne pepper
6 6-ounce trout fillets
½ cup (1 stick) butter

½ cup toasted pecans, chopped
Lemon wedges and fresh parsley (garnish)

For pecan butter: Finely grind pecans in processor or blender. Add butter, Worcestershire and lemon juice and blend well.

For sauce: Heat oil in heavy 2-quart saucepan over medium-high heat. Remove from heat and whisk in flour. Return to heat and cook, stirring constantly, until medium brown, about 10 minutes. Gradually whisk in stock and bring to boil, stirring constantly. Reduce heat to low and simmer until liquid is reduced to 1 cup, about 30 minutes. Increase heat to medium. Gradually whisk in butter and Worcestershire, whisking constantly until butter is completely incorporated. Add parsley, lemon juice, salt and pepper and blend well. Remove sauce from heat and keep warm.

For trout: Beat milk and eggs in medium bowl. Combine flour, garlic powder, salt, pepper and cayenne in large bowl and mix well. Dredge trout fillets in flour mixture, covering completely. Dip trout into milk mixture, then dredge again in flour. Melt butter in large skillet over medium-high heat. Add trout (in batches if necessary) and sauté until golden brown, turning once; do not overcook.

Transfer fillets to heated serving plates. Spread each fillet with enough pecan butter to cover top (about 1 generous tablespoon each). Sprinkle with chopped pecans. Spoon some of sauce over. Garnish with lemon wedges and parsley. Serve immediately, passing remaining sauce separately.

Shellfish

Cajun Calamari

4 servings

¼ cup vegetable oil
1 cup chopped green onion
2 tablespoons soy sauce
½ teaspoon sugar
1 garlic clove, minced
1 pound squid, cleaned and sliced into ¼-inch-thick rings

Salt and freshly ground white pepper
Freshly cooked rice

Heat oil in heavy medium skillet over medium-low heat. Stir in green onion, soy sauce, sugar and garlic. Add squid and simmer until tender, stirring occasionally, about 25 minutes.

Season squid with salt and white pepper. Serve with rice.

Crab Cakes with Creole Sauce

The sauce is a Louisiana favorite that can be used to enhance other seafood.

6 servings

Creole Sauce
¼ cup horseradish
¼ cup fresh lemon juice
2 tablespoons minced green onion
2 tablespoons minced celery
2 tablespoons minced green bell pepper
2 garlic cloves, pureed
1 tablespoon minced fresh parsley
½ teaspoon salt
Freshly ground pepper
½ cup olive oil
Hot pepper sauce
Dried red pepper flakes

Crab Cakes
1 egg

3 tablespoons whipping cream
1 teaspoon dry mustard
½ teaspoon salt
¼ teaspoon cayenne pepper
2 dashes hot pepper sauce
Freshly ground pepper
1 tablespoon minced fresh parsley
1 pound crabmeat, flaked
1½ tablespoons all purpose flour

¼ cup (½ stick) butter
Lemon wedges
Parsley sprigs

For sauce: Mix first 9 ingredients in medium bowl. Whisk in oil in thin stream. Add hot pepper sauce and pepper flakes to taste. (*Can be prepared 1 day ahead. Cover and refrigerate.*)

For crab cakes: Beat first 7 ingredients in medium bowl. Stir in parsley. Mix crabmeat and flour, then combine with egg mixture. Form into twelve 2 × ½-inch round cakes.

Heat butter in heavy large skillet over medium-high heat until light brown. Add crab cakes in batches (do not crowd) and cook until golden brown, about 4 minutes on each side. Drain on paper towels. Arrange on plates. Garnish with lemon and parsley and serve, passing sauce separately.

Baltimore Crab Imperial

4 servings

4 tablespoons (½ stick) unsalted butter
1 small yellow onion, minced
2 tablespoons all purpose flour
⅛ teaspoon cayenne pepper
⅛ teaspoon freshly ground white pepper
⅛ teaspoon ground mace
½ cup milk

½ cup half and half
2 tablespoons dry Sherry
½ cup mayonnaise
   Juice of ½ lemon
   Salt to taste

1 pound lump crabmeat
   Paprika

Preheat oven to 450°F. Melt 2 tablespoons butter in heavy small saucepan over medium heat. Add onion and stir until very lightly browned, about 5 to 8 minutes. Blend in flour, cayenne, white pepper and mace and stir 1 to 2 minutes. Add milk, half and half and Sherry and cook until thick and smooth, about 3 to 4 minutes. Remove from heat. Stir in mayonnaise, lemon juice and salt. Set aside.

Melt remaining 2 tablespoons butter in heavy large skillet over medium heat. Add crab and cook 1 minute, being careful not to break up chunks. Gently fold sauce into crab. Spoon mixture into 5- or 6-cup au gratin dish. (*Recipe can be prepared 2 to 3 hours ahead to this point. Cover tightly with foil and refrigerate immediately.*) Sprinkle top lightly with paprika. Bake until mixture is bubbling and lightly browned, about 12 to 15 minutes. (If crab has been prepared ahead and chilled, cooking time may increase to 20 to 25 minutes.) Serve immediately.

A Raft of Mussels

From the Captain Whidbey, a restaurant in Coupeville, Washington.

6 servings

36 large mussels, scrubbed and debearded

¾ cup (1½ sticks) butter
⅓ cup dry white wine (preferably California Chablis)

½ teaspoon dried basil, crumbled
½ teaspoon paprika

6 romaine leaves
6 large slices French bread, toasted
   Tomato wedges and black olives

Arrange mussels hinge side down in large straight-sided pot. Add ¼ inch water. Cover and cook over high heat just until shells open, about 4 to 5 minutes; do not overcook. Discard any unopened mussels. Remove mussels from shells and set aside. (Mussels can be prepared ahead to this point and refrigerated.)

Melt butter in large skillet over medium heat. Stir in wine, basil and paprika. Add mussels and cook, stirring occasionally, until just heated through.

Arrange romaine leaves on individual plates and top each with slice of toast and some of mussels. Garnish with tomato wedges and black olives.

Beachway Oyster Fritters

Serve with a variety of condiments, such as Dijon mustard, catsup, tartar sauce, cocktail sauce and horseradish.

Makes about 8

½ cup plus 2 tablespoons self-rising flour
½ cup all purpose flour
½ teaspoon salt
¼ teaspoon freshly ground pepper
2 eggs

2½ to 3 cups well-drained shucked oysters (reserve oyster liquor)

Peanut oil (for frying)

Sift flours, salt and pepper; set aside. Beat eggs in large bowl until well blended, about 1 minute. Stir in oysters. Fold in sifted dry ingredients. Gently stir in enough reserved oyster liquor (not more than ½ cup) to make thick batter. Set aside.

Pour peanut oil into heavy large skillet to depth of ¼ inch. Place over medium-high heat. Add batter to hot oil in batches, using about ⅓ cup for each fritter and adding more oil to skillet each time. Fry until golden brown on bottom, then turn and cook second side until tester inserted in centers comes out clean (fritters will flatten to plump patty shape). Drain well on paper towels and serve.

Scallops Chesapeake

4 servings

2 tablespoons (¼ stick) butter
8 ounces mushrooms, sliced
2 teaspoons snipped fresh chives
Pinch *each* of salt and freshly ground pepper

1 pound fresh sea scallops, sliced into ¼-inch discs
½ cup whipping cream
¼ cup brandy

Melt butter in large skillet over high heat. Add mushrooms and sauté until tender, about 2 minutes. Sprinkle with chives, salt and pepper. Add scallops and sauté just until opaque, 2 to 3 minutes. Transfer scallops and mushrooms to 4 large scallop shells or ramekins using slotted spoon; keep warm. Boil pan juices until reduced by half. Add cream and boil until reduced by half, stirring constantly. Heat brandy in small saucepan and ignite, shaking pan until flames subside. Blend brandy into sauce. Spoon over scallop mixture and serve.

Shrimp Chippewa

From Mr. B's Bistro in New Orleans's French Quarter.

6 to 8 servings

1½ cups (3 sticks) butter, cut into ½-inch pieces
56 medium shrimp, shelled (about 2½ pounds)
1½ cups sliced fresh mushrooms
4 garlic cloves, chopped

7 cups boiling chicken stock, preferably homemade
1¼ cups chopped green onion
¼ cup chopped fresh parsley
French bread

Melt ½ cup butter in heavy large saucepan over medium-high heat. Add shrimp, mushrooms and garlic and sauté just until shrimp are pink, about 1 minute; do not overcook. Stir in boiling stock, green onion and parsley. Remove from heat and add remaining 1 cup butter, whisking until melted. Ladle into heated bowls. Serve immediately with French bread.

Acadian Peppered Shrimp

Serve with slices of French bread to soak up the buttery sauce. The quantity of pepper, while surprising, is correct.

8 servings

3 cups (6 sticks) butter
1/2 cup freshly ground pepper
1/4 cup fresh lemon juice
5 medium garlic cloves, minced
4 bay leaves, crumbled
4 teaspoons minced fresh rosemary or 1 1/4 teaspoons dried, crumbled
1 tablespoon Hungarian sweet paprika
1 tablespoon minced fresh basil or 1 teaspoon dried, crumbled

1 tablespoon minced fresh oregano or 1 teaspoon dried, crumbled
1 teaspoon salt
1 teaspoon cayenne pepper
1 teaspoon freshly grated nutmeg
6 pounds whole fresh medium or large shrimp in shell, heads removed

Melt butter in heavy large skillet over medium heat. Add remaining ingredients except shrimp and cook 20 minutes, stirring occasionally. Add shrimp and cook until just pink. Ladle shrimp and sauce into bowls and serve.

Corn Crepes with Shrimp, Green Chilies and Cream

This rich and piquant dish can be prepared one day ahead.

6 servings

Cream Sauce
2 tablespoons (1/4 stick) butter
2 4-ounce cans diced green chilies, drained
1/2 cup minced green onion
1/4 teaspoon minced garlic
2 tablespoons all purpose flour
1 cup chicken stock
1 cup whipping cream
1 cup sour cream, room temperature
1/4 teaspoon salt
1/4 teaspoon freshly ground pepper

1 1/2 pounds medium shrimp, peeled and deveined
2 1/2 cups grated sharp cheddar cheese (9 1/2 ounces)

Corn Crepes*

2 tablespoons minced green onion

For sauce: Melt butter in heavy large saucepan over medium-low heat. Add chilies, 1/2 cup green onion and garlic. Cook until onion is soft, stirring occasionally, about 5 minutes. Add flour and stir 3 minutes. Mix in stock. Increase heat and bring mixture to boil, stirring constantly. Reduce heat and simmer until sauce is smooth, stirring frequently, 3 to 5 minutes. Add cream and simmer until thick, about 2 minutes. Stir in sour cream, salt and pepper. Remove from heat.

Set aside 6 shrimp for garnish. Coarsely dice remainder. Combine diced shrimp, 1 cup sauce and 1 cup cheese in medium bowl.

Generously butter 8 1/2 × 14-inch baking dish. Spoon 2 tablespoons shrimp mixture across lower third of crepe. Roll up, tucking ends under. Arrange seam side down in prepared dish. Repeat with remaining crepes. (*Can be prepared 1 day ahead. Cover and refrigerate. Let stand at room temperature for 1 hour before continuing.*)

Position rack in upper third of oven and preheat to 350°F. Rewarm remaining sauce over medium heat, stirring constantly; do not boil. Pour over crepes. Sprinkle with remaining 1 1/2 cups cheese. Bake 15 minutes. Press reserved shrimp into sauce. Bake until shrimp turn opaque, about 5 minutes. Let cool 5 minutes. Garnish with 2 tablespoons green onion and serve.

*Corn Crepes

Makes about 14

1¼ cups milk
¾ cup yellow cornmeal
2 eggs
⅓ cup all purpose flour

1 teaspoon sugar
¼ teaspoon salt
4 tablespoons (½ stick) butter, melted

Blend milk, cornmeal, eggs, flour, sugar, salt and 2 tablespoons butter in blender or processor until smooth. Let mixture stand for 20 minutes.

Heat 6-inch crepe pan or heavy skillet over medium-high heat. Brush with some of remaining butter. Stir batter. Remove pan from heat and ladle 3 tablespoons batter into corner of pan, tilting pan so batter covers bottom. Return excess batter to bowl. Cook crepe until bottom is golden brown. Turn crepe over and cook until second side is speckled, about 10 seconds. Slide out onto plate. Repeat with remaining batter, adjusting heat as necessary. (*Can be prepared 1 day ahead. Stack crepes between sheets of waxed paper, cover and refrigerate.*)

Tollgate Hill Shellfish Pie

8 appetizer or 4 main-course servings

2 tablespoons (¼ stick) unsalted butter
3 tablespoons finely chopped shallots
1 pound mushrooms, thinly sliced
⅓ cup dry Sherry
2 tablespoons all purpose flour
2 cups whipping cream
¼ teaspoon paprika

1 egg yolk, room temperature
Salt and freshly ground pepper

16 small cherrystone clams, shelled
8 ounces crabmeat
8 ounces uncooked medium shrimp, peeled and deveined
8 ounces bay scallops
8 ounces lobster meat
8 ounces puff pastry
1 egg, beaten to blend (glaze)

Preheat oven to 425°F. Melt butter in heavy large saucepan over medium heat. Add shallots and sauté until slightly softened, about 3 minutes. Add mushrooms and sauté until slightly softened, about 3 minutes. Stir in Sherry. Cook until reduced by half. Reduce heat to medium-low, add flour and stir 3 minutes. Blend in cream and paprika. Increase heat and boil gently until sauce is very thick.

Whisk ¼ cup sauce into yolk. Whisk back into saucepan. Season generously with salt and pepper. Pat shellfish dry. Stir into sauce. Divide mixture among 8 small or 4 larger ramekins, or pour into 1-quart baking dish; do not fill to top. Roll pastry out on lightly floured surface to thickness of ⅛ to ¼ inch. Cover ramekins or dish with pastry, pinching edges to seal. Brush with glaze. Bake until pastry is puffed and golden brown, about 15 minutes. Serve pie immediately.

Southern Seafood Gumbo

Serve with hot garlic bread and dry white wine. If you like a thicker gumbo, add a little more filé powder.

Makes about 3 quarts

½ cup bacon drippings
½ cup all purpose flour
2½ cups chopped onion
1½ cups chopped celery
¾ cup chopped green onion
½ cup chopped green bell pepper
¼ cup chopped fresh parsley
2 medium garlic cloves, minced

1 quart chicken stock
2 cups water
2 cups dry white wine
1 14½-ounce can tomatoes, drained and chopped
¼ cup catsup
1 bay leaf
¾ teaspoon filé powder
½ teaspoon salt
½ teaspoon chopped fresh chervil

⅛ teaspoon dried thyme, crumbled
⅛ teaspoon dried rosemary, crumbled
⅛ teaspoon dried oregano, crumbled
⅛ teaspoon dried basil, crumbled
⅛ teaspoon dried sage, crumbled
⅛ teaspoon chopped fresh tarragon
⅛ teaspoon chopped fresh dill

1 pound fresh shrimp, peeled and deveined
2 cups sliced fresh okra
1 cup fresh bay scallops
8 oysters, shucked, with liquor
6 small clams in shells
½ cup chopped cooked chicken
½ cup chopped fresh ocean perch
½ cup flaked fresh crabmeat

Melt bacon drippings in 5-quart Dutch oven over medium heat. Add flour and stir until copper color, about 15 minutes. Add onion, celery, green onion, green pepper, parsley and garlic and cook 1 hour, stirring frequently to prevent sticking.

Add stock, water, wine, tomatoes, catsup, bay leaf, filé powder, salt and herbs. Cook 1½ hours, stirring occasionally.

Blend in all remaining ingredients and cook 40 minutes. Discard bay leaf. Serve gumbo immediately.

Seafood Filé Gumbo

Roux is the most important component in a successful gumbo. It cannot be rushed and must not burn while cooking or the dish will have a bitter taste.

8 to 10 servings

3 tablespoons butter
1 large onion, chopped
½ cup chopped bell pepper
½ cup chopped celery
4 garlic cloves, minced

½ cup bacon drippings
½ cup all purpose flour
4 quarts chicken stock

2 pounds medium shrimp, peeled (heads and shells reserved)
5 to 6 sprigs fresh thyme or 2 teaspoons dried, crumbled
3 sprigs parsley
2 bay leaves

1 teaspoon freshly ground pepper
1 teaspoon cayenne pepper
Salt

1 pound redfish or sea bass, boned, skinned and cut into bite-size pieces
8 ounces backfin lump crabmeat or Dungeness crab
1 tablespoon filé powder

5 cups freshly cooked rice
Thinly sliced green onions
Minced fresh parsley

Melt butter in heavy large skillet over low heat. Add onion, chopped pepper, celery and garlic. Cover and cook until tender, stirring occasionally, about 5 minutes. Set vegetables aside.

Melt bacon drippings in heavy large saucepan (preferably cast iron) over medium heat. Reduce heat to low. Add flour and stir with wooden spoon until roux is hazelnut color, 30 to 45 minutes. Mix in vegetables and stock. Increase heat; bring to boil, stirring constantly. Reduce heat to medium low.

Wrap reserved shrimp heads and shells, thyme, parsley and bay leaves in square of cheesecloth, tying with twine. Add to saucepan. Season gumbo with pepper, cayenne and salt to taste. Simmer for 1 hour.

Increase heat to medium. Stir in shrimp, redfish and crabmeat and cook 15 minutes. Remove from heat. Adjust seasoning. Blend in filé powder. Let gumbo stand for 5 minutes.

Place ½ cup rice in bottom of each soup bowl. Ladle gumbo over. Garnish with green onions and parsley and serve.

Fisherman's Wharf Cioppino

This is a simple dish to prepare, although it is a good idea to keep a watchful eye on the cooking times toward the end so the fresh seafood does not overcook.

6 servings

3 tablespoons vegetable oil
1 onion, chopped
1 green bell pepper, seeded and chopped
½ cup sliced green onion
4 garlic cloves, minced
4 small tomatoes, peeled, seeded, juiced and chopped
1⅓ cups fresh tomato puree
½ teaspoon chopped fresh thyme or ¼ teaspoon dried, crumbled
1 bay leaf

1 teaspoon salt
¼ teaspoon freshly ground pepper

2 cups dry white wine
6 fresh small clams in shell
6 fresh shrimp, shelled and deveined
6 fresh scallops
6 fresh crab legs, disjointed
2 fresh lobster tails, quartered and cracked

Heat oil in large skillet over medium-high heat. Add onion, green pepper, green onion and garlic and sauté just until softened, about 5 minutes. Add tomato, tomato puree, thyme, bay leaf, salt and pepper. Increase heat and bring to boil. Reduce heat to low, cover and simmer 2 hours, stirring occasionally.

Add wine. Increase heat to high and bring to boil. Reduce heat to low and simmer 15 minutes. Place seafood in large stockpot. Pour vegetable mixture over. Bring to boil over high heat. Reduce heat to low, cover and simmer until fish is cooked, removing each with slotted spoon as it is done, about 10 to 15 minutes total (depending on size of fish). Divide seafood among individual shallow bowls. Ladle vegetable mixture over each portion and serve immediately.

Massachusetts Fish Stew

4 servings

⅓ cup olive oil
½ cup chopped onion
5 small garlic cloves, minced
5 tablespoons minced fresh parsley
1 teaspoon dried basil, crumbled
1 teaspoon dried oregano, crumbled
½ teaspoon ground saffron or turmeric
1 1-pound can Italian plum tomatoes, undrained

⅔ cup dry white wine
1½ pounds cod or haddock, cut into ¾-inch chunks
8 ounces bay scallops, halved
1 6½-ounce can minced clams, undrained
Salt and freshly ground pepper
Italian bread

Heat oil in large saucepan over medium heat. Add onion and garlic and sauté until onion is soft, about 5 minutes. Stir in parsley, basil, oregano and saffron. Add tomatoes with liquid and wine and simmer 5 minutes. Stir in fish, scallops and clams with liquid and simmer until fish is tender, about 20 minutes. Season with salt and pepper. Serve with bread.

7 ❦ Vegetables, Side Dishes and Salads

Vegetables spilling forth from a cornucopia are the very symbol of abundance. This chapter celebrates the bounty of the American harvest, from New England's hardy root vegetables to the avocados and chilies of the sun-drenched Southwest.

Some of these dishes are substantial enough to serve as main courses—among them Black Bean Chili (page 74), Cajun-Style Seafood Eggplant (page 76), Heron's Stuffed Potato Skins (page 80), and Fried Green Tomatoes with Bacon Cream (page 81). Others, such as Green Beans with Chilies and Cilantro (page 75), Baked Desert Vegetables (page 77), and Pear and Turnip Puree (page 77), make flavorful accompaniments to meat, poultry or fish entrées.

There is also an appealing collection of heritage dishes for the holidays, particularly the most American of them all, Thanksgiving. Choose from Maple-Glazed Carrots, Parsnips and Rutabaga (page 76), Butternut Squash with Leeks and Apples (page 79), Baked Yam Stew with Dried Fruit (page 78), Wild Rice with Sausage and Mushrooms (page 82)—all perfect complements to the centerpiece roast or turkey.

Not to be overlooked is the selection of unusual composed salads. Again, some are perfect as a light meal—think of the classic American spinach salad, garnished variously with bacon, egg, mushrooms, cheese and avocado. Other salads in this chapter make great appetizers or side dishes, and the dressings are terrific with whatever fixings are freshest and most plentiful at the market.

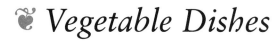 Vegetable Dishes

Black Bean Chili

8 servings

1 pound dried black beans

2 tablespoons olive oil
1½ cups chopped onion
2 tablespoons chopped seeded fresh
   green chilies
2 teaspoons minced garlic
2 teaspoons ground cumin
1 teaspoon ground coriander
1 teaspoon chili powder
½ teaspoon dried red pepper flakes

7 cups water
1 1-pound can tomatoes
   (undrained), chopped
¾ teaspoon salt

1 tablespoon tequila (optional)
1 tablespoon red wine vinegar
   Crème fraîche or sour cream
   Minced fresh cilantro or parsley

Soak beans overnight in water to cover generously.

Heat oil in Dutch oven or heavy large saucepan over medium-high heat. Add onion, 1½ tablespoons chilies and 1½ teaspoons garlic and stir 1 minute. Mix in cumin, coriander, chili powder and red pepper flakes and sauté 30 seconds. Mix in 7 cups water and tomatoes. Drain beans and add to soup. Bring to boil. Reduce heat, cover and simmer, stirring occasionally, until beans are very soft, about 3½ hours. Stir in ¾ teaspoon salt.

Puree half of soup in processor until smooth. Return to pan. (*Can be prepared 2 days ahead to this point. Cool, cover and refrigerate. Reheat before continuing, thinning with more water if necessary.*) Stir in remaining ½ tablespoon green chilies and ½ teaspoon garlic. Simmer 15 minutes to blend flavors.

Just before serving, stir in tequila and vinegar. Taste and adjust seasoning. Spoon into bowls. Top with crème fraîche and cilantro.

Blue Ribbon Pinto Beans

These are also excellent re-fried: Mash, then fry in a small amount of lard.

10 servings

2 pounds dried pinto beans
1 pound sliced smoked bacon, cut
   into 1-inch pieces
2 medium tomatoes, diced
1½ tablespoons ground cumin

1½ tablespoons chili powder
2 medium garlic cloves, minced
1 serrano or jalapeño pepper,
   minced
   Salt

Place beans in heavy large saucepan. Cover with water and bring to boil. Drain. Return beans to pan. Pour in water to cover by 2 to 3 inches. Add all remaining ingredients except salt. Bring mixture to boil. Reduce heat to low and simmer until beans are very soft, adding more water as necessary to keep beans submerged, about 3½ hours. Season with salt and cook 15 minutes longer, uncovered, if beans are too liquid. Let cool. Chill overnight. To serve, reheat beans over medium-low heat, stirring frequently.

Barbecued Limas

The "barbecue" flavor comes from the seasonings. Great with any dinner.

8 servings

1 pound shelled fresh lima beans or 1 pound frozen

4 ounces bacon, cut into ¼-inch pieces
1 medium onion, chopped
1 medium-size green bell pepper, chopped

1 15-ounce can tomato sauce
1 14½-ounce can stewed tomatoes
1 teaspoon salt

½ cup grated Monterey Jack cheese

Cover lima beans with cold water in large saucepan. Bring to boil, skimming surface. Simmer until tender, adding more water if necessary, about 25 minutes for fresh or 5 to 6 minutes for frozen. Drain thoroughly.

Grease 12-inch gratin pan or deep casserole. Cook bacon in heavy 10-inch skillet over medium-low heat until translucent, about 10 minutes. Add onion and green pepper and cook until tender, stirring frequently, about 10 minutes. Add beans and cook until hot, stirring frequently, about 5 minutes. Mix in tomato sauce and stewed tomatoes. Cover and simmer 15 minutes. Uncover and simmer until most of tomato juice is absorbed, stirring frequently, about 20 minutes. Mix in salt. Pour into dish. (*Can be prepared 1 day ahead and refrigerated. Bring to room temperature before continuing.*)

Preheat oven to 450°F. Sprinkle cheese over beans. Bake until beans are heated through and cheese melts, about 20 minutes. Serve immediately.

Green Beans with Vermont Smoked Ham

8 servings

1½ pounds green beans, trimmed

¼ cup olive oil
4 ounces Vermont smoked ham or Black Forest ham, finely chopped
¼ cup minced shallot

6 tablespoons minced fresh parsley
¼ cup chopped toasted almonds
3 medium garlic cloves, minced
Freshly ground pepper

Cook beans in large amount of rapidly boiling salted water until crisp-tender, about 4 minutes. Rinse and drain.

Heat oil in heavy large skillet over medium heat. Sauté ham and shallot until just light brown, about 2 minutes. Add beans and remaining ingredients and sauté until hot. Serve immediately.

Green Beans with Chilies and Cilantro

8 servings

1½ pounds green beans

3 tablespoons fresh lime juice
½ cup (1 stick) unsalted butter, room temperature

Salt and freshly ground pepper
¼ cup minced cilantro
2 small hot green chilies, seeded and minced

If beans are large, cut diagonally into 2-inch lengths. Bring large amount of salted water to rapid boil. Add beans and cook until crisp-tender. Drain and plunge into ice water to cool quickly and set color. Drain well; pat dry.

Blend lime juice into butter. Season with salt and pepper. Mix cilantro and chilies in another bowl.

To serve, reheat beans in large skillet over medium heat. Remove from heat. Toss with lime butter to coat. Sprinkle with cilantro mixture.

Maple-Glazed Carrots, Parsnips and Rutabaga

8 to 10 servings

1 pound carrots, peeled and cut into 3 × 1/4-inch strips
1 pound parsnips, peeled and cut into 3 × 1/4-inch strips
1 pound rutabaga, peeled and cut into 3 × 1/4-inch strips

6 tablespoons (3/4 stick) unsalted butter, room temperature

2 tablespoons fresh lemon juice
2 tablespoons maple syrup
1 1/4 teaspoons salt
1/4 teaspoon cinnamon
Freshly ground pepper

Steam vegetables until crisp-tender, about 8 minutes. (*Can be prepared 2 days ahead, cooled, covered and refrigerated. Reheat gently before continuing.*)

Combine remaining ingredients in large bowl. Add vegetables and toss gently. Adjust seasoning. Serve hot.

Feelings Cafe Cajun-Style Seafood Baked Eggplant

8 to 10 servings

1/2 cup (1 stick) butter
4 ounces hot link sausage, diced
4 ounces chicken gizzards, diced
3 medium eggplants, peeled and diced
3 green bell peppers, seeded and chopped
3 medium onions, chopped
2 garlic cloves, minced
1 bunch green onions, chopped
1/2 cup chopped celery
8 ounces fresh small shrimp, shelled and deveined

1 cup cooked rice
1/4 cup chopped fresh parsley
1 teaspoon Italian seasoning
Salt

8 ounces lump crabmeat
1/3 to 1/2 cup Italian breadcrumbs
2 to 3 tablespoons butter
Lemon slices and chopped fresh parsley (garnish)

Melt 1/2 cup butter in Dutch oven or large saucepan over medium-high heat. Add sausage and gizzards and sauté until browned, about 5 minutes. Stir in eggplant, bell pepper, onion, garlic, green onion and celery and continue to cook, stirring occasionally, about 15 minutes. Add shrimp, rice, parsley, Italian seasoning and salt. Cook, stirring occasionally, until shrimp is pink and translucent, about 15 minutes. Remove from heat.

Preheat oven to 350°F. Add crabmeat to eggplant mixture with enough breadcrumbs to absorb remaining butter. Spoon into individual ramekins. Sprinkle with remaining breadcrumbs and dot with butter. Bake until tops are browned. Garnish with lemon and parsley. Serve immediately.

Fried Okra

12 servings

2 cups cornmeal
2 teaspoons salt
3 pounds fresh okra, washed,

stemmed and cut crosswise into 1/2-inch-thick slices
4 cups peanut oil (for deep frying)

Combine cornmeal and salt on plate. Dredge okra in mixture. Heat oil in large saucepan or deep-fat fryer to 375°F. Fry okra in batches until browned. Drain thoroughly on paper towels. Serve immediately.

Baked Desert Vegetables

6 servings

2 tablespoons (¼ stick) butter
2 tablespoons olive oil
1 medium onion, thinly sliced
14 ounces zucchini, sliced crosswise
     ¼ inch thick
4½ teaspoons fresh chervil or
     1½ teaspoons dried, crumbled

Salt and freshly ground pepper
Kernels from 5 large ears of corn
3 medium-size red bell peppers,
     halved lengthwise, cored and
     seeded
6 teaspoons breadcrumbs
2 to 3 tablespoons butter

Preheat oven to 400°F. Heat 2 tablespoons butter with oil in heavy large skillet over medium-high heat. Add onion and sauté just until softened. Stir in zucchini, chervil, salt and pepper and sauté until zucchini is crisp-tender; add corn. Meanwhile, blanch peppers in boiling salted water 4 minutes. Drain and rinse under cold water; pat dry. Set peppers on baking sheet. Fill evenly with vegetables. Sprinkle each with 1 teaspoon breadcrumbs and dot with remaining butter. Bake until heated through, about 10 minutes. Serve immediately.

Pear and Turnip Puree

10 servings

4 ounces dried pears
½ medium lemon, cut into 4 pieces
1 1½-inch cinnamon stick
5 large firm pears (such as Bosc),
     peeled and quartered

3 pounds turnips, peeled and cut
     into 1½-inch cubes

6 tablespoons (¾ stick) unsalted
     butter, room temperature
½ cup whipping cream, room
     temperature
Salt and freshly ground white
     pepper
Freshly grated nutmeg

Combine dried pears, lemon, cinnamon and water to cover in heavy medium saucepan and bring to simmer. Cook until pears are very soft, about 20 minutes. Add fresh pears and simmer until tender, about 10 minutes.

   Cook turnips in gently simmering water until tender, about 10 minutes.

   Drain pears and turnips. Pat both dry. Transfer to processor and puree using on/off turns. Add butter and blend well. With machine running, add cream through feed tube. Turn out into heated dish and serve immediately. (*Can be prepared 1 day ahead and reheated gently in double boiler.*)

Mother Edel's Shredded Yam Casserole

These sweet and slightly crisp yams would be a nice accompaniment to ham or pork. Stirring them into salted water helps remove excess starch.

10 servings

1 gallon cold water
1 teaspoon salt
2 pounds yams, peeled and
     shredded
½ cup sugar

½ cup light corn syrup
¼ cup water
¼ cup (½ stick) butter
1 cup unsweetened pineapple juice
Freshly grated nutmeg

Preheat oven to 350°F. Grease 9 × 13-inch baking dish. Combine 1 gallon cold water and salt in large saucepan. Stir in yams; drain well. Turn into prepared dish. Heat sugar, corn syrup and ¼ cup water in heavy large saucepan over low heat until sugar dissolves, swirling pan occasionally. Increase heat and boil until syrup is consistency of heavy cream, about 7 minutes. Remove from heat. Stir in butter until melted. Pour pineapple juice over yams, then syrup. Sprinkle with nutmeg. Bake until tender, about 1 hour. Let stand 5 minutes before serving.

Baked Yam Stew with Dried Fruit

Delicious with beef, lamb or poultry.

4 servings

²⁄₃ cup dried apricots (about 2 ounces)

³⁄₄ cup pitted prunes (about 4 ounces)

3 tablespoons unsalted butter
1 large yam (about 1½ pounds), peeled, halved lengthwise and cut into ½-inch slices
Salt and freshly ground pepper

3 long white boiling potatoes (about 1 pound total), peeled and cut crosswise into ½-inch slices
Salt

½ cup strained fresh orange juice
¼ cup honey
2 tablespoons (¼ stick) unsalted butter
1 tablespoon strained fresh lemon juice
½ teaspoon cinnamon
Small pinch of ground cloves

1 tablespoon vegetable oil
½ cup whole blanched almonds

Place apricots and prunes in separate bowls. Cover each fruit with boiling water and let soak until almost tender, about 30 minutes for apricots and about 35 minutes for prunes.

Preheat oven to 400°F. Melt 3 tablespoons butter in 2-quart baking dish in oven. Add yam and season with salt and pepper; toss to coat with butter. Bake until just tender, stirring occasionally, about 25 minutes.

Meanwhile, combine potatoes and pinch of salt with water to cover in medium saucepan. Bring to boil. Reduce heat, cover and simmer until just tender, about 15 minutes. Drain well.

Drain apricots and prunes. Gently mix into yams. Stir in potatoes. Bring orange juice, honey, 2 tablespoons butter, lemon juice, cinnamon and cloves to simmer in heavy small saucepan, stirring constantly. Pour over stew. Bake 15 minutes, basting twice. Using rubber spatula, gently stir, bringing bottom ingredients to top. Continue baking until liquid is reduced to about ⅓ cup, basting 3 times, about 10 minutes. (*Can be prepared 4 hours ahead. Cover and let stand at room temperature. Reheat covered in 300°F oven.*)

Heat oil in heavy large skillet over medium-low heat. Add almonds and pinch of salt. Stir until light brown, about 4 minutes. Sprinkle over stew and serve.

Yam and Butternut Squash Pudding

This new twist on favorite holiday vegetables has a velvety texture.

10 servings

1 1½-pound butternut squash
1½ pounds yams

1 cup milk
1 cup whipping cream
6 eggs, room temperature
½ cup firmly packed light brown sugar

1 teaspoon cinnamon
½ teaspoon freshly grated nutmeg
½ teaspoon salt

Preheat oven to 400°F. Bake squash and yams until soft, about 1 hour. Cool to room temperature.

Peel squash; discard seeds. Puree pulp in processor until smooth. Transfer 1½ cups to mixer bowl. Peel yams. Puree in processor until smooth. Add 1½ cups to squash. Beat remaining ingredients into mixture. (*Can be prepared 1 day ahead and refrigerated. Bring to room temperature before continuing.*)

Preheat oven to 350°F. Grease 6- or 7-cup soufflé dish. Pour pudding into dish. Place in roasting pan. Add enough hot water to roasting pan to come 1½ inches up side of soufflé dish. Bake until pudding is firm to touch, about 1½ hours. Serve hot.

Butternut Squash with Leeks and Apples

6 servings

½ cup fresh parsley leaves
4 large shallots

1 large leek (including green part), cut into processor feed-tube lengths

1 2-pound butternut squash, peeled, seeded and cut to fit processor feed tube
¼ cup (½ stick) unsalted butter

1 Granny Smith apple, peeled, halved, cored and sides cut flat
1½ tablespoons maple syrup
1 teaspoon salt
½ teaspoon freshly grated nutmeg
Freshly ground pepper

Mince parsley in processor using on/off turns. Remove from work bowl and set aside. With machine running, drop shallots through feed tube and mince.

Insert thick or medium slicer into processor. Stand leek in feed tube; slice using medium pressure.

Using medium slicer, place squash in feed tube and slice using firm pressure. Melt butter in heavy 10-inch skillet over medium heat. Stir in shallots, leek and squash. Cover and cook until crisp-tender, about 8 minutes.

Place apple in feed tube, flat side down, and slice using medium pressure. Add apple, maple syrup, salt, nutmeg and pepper to skillet and toss lightly to combine. Cook until apples soften slightly, stirring occasionally, about 4 minutes. Stir in parsley. Adjust seasoning and serve.

Acorn Squash with Nut-Crumb Topping

8 servings

1 large acorn squash, halved through stem end, seeds discarded

¼ cup (½ stick) unsalted butter
¼ cup maple syrup or liquid brown sugar

1 tablespoon dry breadcrumbs
½ cup coarsely chopped walnuts or pecans

Position rack in center of oven and preheat to 350°F. Place squash cut side down in roasting pan. Pour enough cold water into pan to come ½ inch up sides. Bake squash until easily pierced with fork, about 40 minutes.

Cut each squash piece lengthwise in half; cut each slice horizontally into 2 wedges. Arrange skin side down on platter and return to turned-off oven. Melt butter in heavy small skillet over medium heat. Mix in maple syrup and breadcrumbs. Add nuts and stir until heated through, about 30 seconds. Spoon evenly over squash and serve.

Country Corn Pudding

4 to 6 servings

¼ cup (½ stick) butter
3 tablespoons all purpose flour
1½ cups milk or half and half

2 eggs
1 tablespoon chopped fresh parsley
1 teaspoon salt

¼ teaspoon cayenne pepper
3 cups corn kernels
Crumbled cooked bacon or cubed ham (optional)

Preheat oven to 350°F. Butter 2-quart baking dish. Melt butter in small skillet over medium-high heat. Add flour and stir until smooth. Cook 1 minute, stirring constantly. Gradually add milk, stirring constantly until sauce is thickened. Remove from heat.

Beat eggs in large bowl. Gradually whisk sauce into eggs, blending well after each addition. Mix in parsley, salt and cayenne. Add corn and mix thoroughly. Turn into baking dish. Sprinkle top with bacon or ham. Bake until top is lightly golden and center is set, about 20 to 30 minutes. Serve immediately.

Heron's Stuffed Potato Skins

Stuffed potato skins have rapidly become a new American classic.

4 servings

4 medium baking potatoes, cooked

8 ounces cheddar cheese, shredded
4 bacon strips, fried until crisp, crumbled
2 egg whites, room temperature
1 2-ounce jar pimientos, diced
2 medium-size green onions, chopped

½ cup fine fresh white breadcrumbs

Oil (for deep frying)
Sour cream
Snipped fresh chives

Cut potatoes in half lengthwise. Scoop out all but ¼ inch pulp; reserve for another use. Set potato shells aside.

Mix cheese, bacon, whites, pimientos and onions until well blended. Pack tightly into potato shells, mounding tops slightly. Sprinkle with breadcrumbs, covering completely.

Preheat oven to 350°F. Heat oil in deep fryer or heavy large saucepan to 350°F. Lower stuffed potatoes into oil and fry until breadcrumbs are golden brown, 40 to 60 seconds. Drain on paper towels. Arrange potatoes in baking pan. Bake until cheese is thoroughly melted, about 15 minutes. Serve immediately with sour cream and chives.

Nutmeg Potato Croquettes

Makes about 12 large croquettes

3 to 4 medium baking potatoes (about 1½ to 1¾ pounds), peeled
¼ cup (½ stick) butter, room temperature
2 tablespoons whipping cream, half and half or milk
2 tablespoons chopped fresh parsley
¼ teaspoon salt

⅛ teaspoon freshly grated nutmeg
⅛ teaspoon freshly ground pepper
½ cup freshly grated Parmesan cheese

⅓ cup (about) all purpose flour
2 eggs, beaten
1 cup fine dry breadcrumbs

Oil (for deep frying)

Cover potatoes with water in large saucepan. Bring to boil over high heat. Reduce heat to medium and simmer until very tender but not mushy, about 30 minutes. Drain well. Transfer potatoes to large bowl of electric mixer. Add butter, cream, parsley, salt, nutmeg and pepper and beat until smooth. Add cheese, blending well. Let cool, then chill several hours or overnight.

By hand or with 2 large spoons, form mixture into potato shapes using about 1/2 cup for each. Gently dredge in flour; coat with egg, then breadcrumbs. Arrange on baking sheet. Chill 1 hour or overnight.

Heat oil for deep frying in large saucepan or wok to 350° F. Add croquettes in batches of 6 and fry until crisp and browned on all sides, about 4 to 5 minutes. Drain well on paper towels. Serve immediately.

New England Fried Green Tomatoes with Bacon Cream

Accompany this tasty regional dish with hot homemade biscuits for dipping into the creamy sauce. Delicious for brunch or a light supper.

6 servings

12 slices thick-cut bacon

1 1/2 cups stone-ground yellow cornmeal

2 eggs

1/4 cup milk

10 green tomatoes, sliced into 1/2-inch rounds

Salt and freshly ground pepper

1 1/2 cups whipping cream

3 tablespoons snipped fresh chives

Cook bacon in heavy large skillet over low heat until lightly crisped. Remove from skillet and keep warm. Strain bacon drippings. Wipe out skillet. Add strained bacon drippings to skillet.

Spread cornmeal on baking sheet. Blend eggs and milk in shallow pie plate. Dip tomato slice into egg mixture. Dredge in cornmeal on both sides, shaking off excess. Set on rack. Repeat with remaining slices. Let stand 5 minutes before frying.

Heat bacon drippings over medium heat. Sauté tomato slices in batches (do not crowd) until golden brown on both sides. Season with salt and pepper. Transfer to heated platter and keep warm.

Pour off all but 1 tablespoon bacon drippings. Stir in cream and cook over medium-high heat until reduced by half. Mix in 2 tablespoons chives. Season with salt and pepper. Ladle sauce over tomatoes. Sprinkle with remaining chives. Crumble reserved bacon over and serve immediately.

❧ *Rice and Grits*

Pecan Pilaf

6 to 8 servings

1/2 cup (1 stick) butter or margarine

1 cup chopped pecans

1/2 cup chopped onion

2 cups long-grain rice

2 cups chicken stock

2 cups water

1/2 teaspoon salt or to taste

1/4 teaspoon dried thyme crumbled

1/8 teaspoon freshly ground pepper

3 tablespoons chopped fresh parsley

Melt 3 tablespoons butter in large skillet over medium-high heat. Add pecans and sauté until lightly browned, about 2 to 3 minutes. Transfer pecans to small bowl using slotted spoon. Cover and set aside. Melt remaining butter in same skillet. Add onion and sauté until tender, about 5 minutes. Add rice and stir until evenly coated, about 2 minutes.

Meanwhile, bring stock, water, salt, thyme, pepper and 2 tablespoons parsley to boil in medium saucepan over medium-high heat. Add to rice. Cover, reduce heat to low and simmer until all liquid is absorbed, about 20 minutes. Add pecans and remaining parsley. Fluff with fork and serve.

Wild Rice with Sausage and Mushrooms

Serve as an accompaniment to pheasant or other poultry. Pork and Veal Sausage can also be formed into patties and fried for breakfast. The double cooking of the rice ensures separate grains that do not stick to each other.

10 to 12 servings

8 ounces long-grain rice	1 teaspoon dried marjoram, crumbled
8 ounces wild rice	1 teaspoon dried thyme, crumbled
3 tablespoons butter	1 teaspoon dried sage, crumbled
1 pound Pork and Veal Sausage*	1 teaspoon fennel seeds
1 pound onions, chopped	1 teaspoon salt
1 pound mushrooms, chopped	

Cook long-grain rice in large pot of boiling water 10 minutes. Drain. Wrap loosely in 2 layers of cheesecloth. Repeat with wild rice, wrapping separately. Bring water to boil in steamer. Set rice packages on steamer rack. Cover and steam until rice is tender, about 20 minutes for long-grain rice and about 50 minutes for wild rice, adding water to steamer as necessary. Unwrap both. Transfer to bowl. Toss lightly with fork to separate. (*Can be prepared 1 day ahead and refrigerated.*)

Melt butter in heavy large skillet over high heat. Add sausage, onions and mushrooms. Cook until sausage is no longer pink, stirring frequently, about 10 minutes. Mix in seasonings and rice.

Preheat oven to 350°F. Butter 3-quart casserole. Add rice mixture. Cook until heated through, about 15 minutes. Serve immediately.

*Pork and Veal Sausage

Makes about 1⅓ pounds

12 ounces trimmed boneless pork loin, ground	1 teaspoon dried sage, crumbled
8 ounces ground veal	¾ teaspoon salt
1 shallot, minced	½ teaspoon dried thyme, crumbled
1 teaspoon fennel seeds	½ teaspoon freshly ground pepper

Mix all ingredients in bowl, using hands. To check seasoning, pinch off small piece of mixture and fry until cooked through. Taste, then adjust seasoning of uncooked portion. (*Can be prepared 2 days ahead and refrigerated.*)

Wild Rice with Hazelnuts

8 servings

4 cups chicken stock	1 cup hazelnuts, toasted and husked
2 cups wild rice, rinsed	Minced fresh parsley
Salt and freshly ground pepper	
3 tablespoons butter	
4 shallots, minced	

Bring stock to boil in saucepan. Stir in rice. Reduce heat, cover and simmer 20 minutes. Uncover and simmer until liquid has evaporated, 20 to 25 minutes. Season with salt and pepper.

Melt butter in heavy small skillet over medium-low heat. Add shallots and cook until softened, stirring occasionally, about 5 minutes. Combine rice, shallots and hazelnuts in bowl. Garnish with parsley. Serve immediately.

Garlic Grits

Grits were never so appealing: These are zesty, rich and creamy.

8 servings

4 cups water
1 teaspoon salt
1 cup quick grits
8 ounces sharp cheddar cheese, grated
½ cup (1 stick) unsalted butter
3 eggs, beaten to blend
⅓ cup milk

2 tablespoons freshly grated Parmesan cheese
1 tablespoon snipped fresh chives
1 tablespoon minced fresh parsley
1 teaspoon minced garlic
Snipped fresh chives (garnish)

Preheat oven to 325°F. Grease 1½-quart soufflé dish. Bring water and salt to boil in heavy medium saucepan. Slowly stir in grits. Cook until water is absorbed, stirring constantly, about 4 minutes. Remove from heat and stir in remaining ingredients except garnish. Spoon into prepared dish. (*Can be prepared 1 hour ahead.*) Bake until knife inserted in center comes out clean, about 1 hour. Top with chives and serve.

Salads and Dressings

Saloon Slaw

Arranging the vegetables separately makes for a particularly attractive presentation—a mini salad bar in a bowl.

6 to 8 servings

12 cups of a combination of any of the following:
Red, green or Chinese cabbage, shredded
Zucchini, thinly sliced
Carrot, shredded
Celery, thinly sliced
Snow peas (strings removed)
Corn kernels (uncooked), cut from cob
Mushrooms, sliced
Red or green bell pepper, thinly sliced

Alfalfa or bean sprouts
Endive, thinly sliced
Daikon or red radish, thinly sliced or shredded
Cucumber, thinly sliced
Tart apple (cored), chopped or thinly sliced
Avocado, peeled, pitted and diced

Sour Cream Dressing*

Place prepared ingredients (except apple and avocado) in individual plastic bags and refrigerate up to 1 day.

Just before serving, arrange ingredients attractively in large salad bowl, adding apple and avocado if using. Pass sour cream dressing at table.

*Sour Cream Dressing

The uncomplicated flavor of yellow "ball park" mustard is just right here.

Makes about 2 cups

³/₄ cup sour cream
³/₄ cup mayonnaise
¹/₂ cup finely minced onion
4¹/₂ teaspoons prepared yellow mustard

1 tablespoon distilled white vinegar
1 tablespoon sugar
¹/₄ teaspoon freshly ground pepper

Blend all ingredients in small bowl. Transfer to container with tight-fitting lid. Cover dressing and refrigerate for at least 2 hours before serving.
Can be stored in refrigerator up to 2 days.

Nancy's Mother's Coleslaw

4 to 6 servings

1 medium onion, chopped
1 cup sugar
1 cup vegetable oil
¹/₂ cup cider vinegar

¹/₃ cup mayonnaise
¹/₂ teaspoon celery seed
1 teaspoon salt
1 medium cabbage, shredded

Combine onion and sugar in medium bowl. Let stand for 30 minutes. Add all remaining ingredients except cabbage and blend well. Cover and refrigerate. Just before serving, add cabbage and toss well.

Jícama, Avocado and Lime Salad with Sour-Sweet Lime Dressing

6 servings

Sour-Sweet Lime Dressing
5 tablespoons fresh lime juice
1 tablespoon orange or lime marmalade
1 teaspoon minced lime peel
¹/₂ teaspoon salt
   Dash of hot pepper sauce
5 tablespoons olive oil

1 1-pound jícama, halved lengthwise and peeled
12 cherry tomatoes
2 avocados, peeled, pitted and sliced
12 Greek or Niçoise olives
1 lime, peeled and finely diced

1 head romaine lettuce

For dressing: Mix first 5 ingredients in small bowl. Whisk in oil in thin stream.
   Line 6 plates with lettuce leaves. Cut jícama lengthwise into ¹/₈-inch-thick slices. Arrange jícama and tomatoes atop lettuce. (*Can be prepared 2 hours ahead. Cover and refrigerate.*) Just before serving, divide avocado and olives among salads. Top with diced lime. Stir dressing and pour over salads.

Fiddlehead Ferns and Leeks with Maple Vinaigrette

6 servings

12 ounces fiddlehead ferns,* trimmed (dry leaves removed)
12 ounces small leeks, trimmed and cut into 4-inch lengths

1 tablespoon Sherry vinegar or red wine vinegar
1 teaspoon Dijon mustard
¹/₃ teaspoon salt
¹/₄ cup walnut oil

1 tablespoon maple syrup
1 teaspoon minced fresh herbs (such as tarragon and chives)
   Freshly ground pepper

1 hard-cooked egg, yolk and white coarsely chopped separately
¹/₄ cup coarsely chopped pecans
¹/₄ cup minced fresh parsley

Cook fiddlehead ferns in large amount of boiling salted water until crisp-tender, about 3 minutes. Rinse with cold water and drain. Split leeks lengthwise and rinse thoroughly. Tie into 2 bundles. Cook in large amount of boiling salted water until tender. Rinse with cold water and drain. Dry fiddleheads and leeks thoroughly. Arrange in alternating rows on platter.

Mix vinegar, mustard and salt in small bowl. Whisk in oil 1 drop at a time. Stir in maple syrup, herbs and generous amount of pepper. Spoon half of vinaigrette over vegetables. Marinate at least 1 hour. (*Can be prepared several hours ahead and refrigerated. Bring to room temperature before serving.*)

Arrange chopped yolk, white, pecans and parsley decoratively around vegetables. Whisk remaining vinaigrette. Spoon over vegetables and serve.

*If unavailable, use 1¼ pounds asparagus, trimmed to 4-inch lengths.

Avocado-Spinach Salad

4 to 6 servings

10 ounces fresh spinach, stemmed and torn into pieces
1 cup seasoned croutons
4 ounces Swiss cheese, cut into ¼-inch strips
4 hard-cooked eggs, quartered

2 avocados, peeled, halved, pitted and sliced crosswise
½ Bermuda onion, thinly sliced
Lemon-Mustard Vinaigrette*

Combine spinach, croutons, cheese, eggs, avocado and onion in large salad bowl and toss gently. Just before serving, shake dressing thoroughly, pour over salad and toss again.

*Lemon-Mustard Vinaigrette

Makes about ¾ cup

½ cup vegetable oil
1½ tablespoons vinegar
1½ tablespoons fresh lemon juice

¼ to ½ teaspoon salt
¼ teaspoon Dijon mustard
Freshly ground pepper

Combine all ingredients in jar with tight-fitting lid and shake well. Refrigerate until ready to use.

Sweet Potato Salad

A fresh variation on the Waldorf salad.

6 servings

¼ cup mayonnaise
2 tablespoons fresh lemon juice
2 tablespoons sugar
½ teaspoon salt
2 large sweet potatoes or yams, cooked in skins

1 cup diced celery
1 cup chopped tart apple
⅓ cup chopped walnuts
6 lettuce leaves

Combine mayonnaise, lemon juice, sugar and salt in large bowl and whisk to blend. Peel potatoes and cut into ½-inch cubes. Add potatoes, celery, apple and nuts to mayonnaise mixture and toss to coat. Cover and refrigerate. Serve chilled salad on lettuce leaves.

Wild Rice, Peas and Mushroom Salad

12 servings

8 ounces fresh mushrooms, thinly sliced
Juice of 1 lemon
8 ounces wild rice, cooked and drained
2 cups fresh green peas (about 2 pounds unshelled), cooked and drained

4 green onions, thinly sliced
¾ cup Vinaigrette*
1 tablespoon finely chopped fresh tarragon or ¼ teaspoon dried, crumbled
¼ teaspoon sugar
Salt and freshly ground pepper

Combine mushrooms and lemon juice in large bowl. And rice, peas and onion. Combine vinaigrette, tarragon and sugar in small bowl and mix well. Add to rice mixture. Toss lightly. Season with salt and pepper and serve immediately.

*Vinaigrette

Makes about ¾ cup

1 small to medium garlic clove, minced
2 teaspoons Dijon mustard
1 teaspoon coarse salt

½ teaspoon freshly ground pepper or to taste
¼ cup white wine vinegar
⅓ to ½ cup vegetable oil

Combine garlic, mustard, salt and pepper in medium bowl. Slowly whisk in vinegar. Gradually add oil, whisking constantly until thoroughly blended.

Winter Vinaigrette

Beef fat drippings are the secret to this pungent dressing. Use with an assortment of slightly bitter greens such as escarole and curly endive.

Makes about 1⅓ cups

1 tablespoon beef fat drippings (see recipe for Plymouth Prime Rib, page 34)
6 shallots, minced
1 small garlic clove, pressed
⅓ cup red wine vinegar

3 tablespoons degreased beef fat drippings (see recipe for Plymouth Prime Rib)
1 teaspoon sugar
⅔ cup olive oil
Salt and freshly ground pepper

Heat 1 tablespoon beef fat drippings in heavy medium skillet over medium heat. Add shallots and garlic and stir until softened, 3 to 4 minutes. Add vinegar, degreased beef fat drippings and sugar and cook 4 minutes. Remove from heat. Whisk in oil in thin stream. Season with salt and pepper.

Peppercorn Dressing

Serve over a mixture of romaine leaves and sliced mushrooms; top the salad with cherry tomato, alfalfa sprouts and crumbled bacon. Hard-cooked egg wedges and crumbled bleu cheese make a perfect garnish.

Makes about 1⅓ cups

¾ cup (generous) sour cream
¼ cup mayonnaise, preferably homemade
2 tablespoons fresh lemon juice
3½ to 4 teaspoons coarsely cracked pepper

1 teaspoon Worcestershire sauce
1 beef bouillon cube dissolved in 4 teaspoons warm water
Pinch of salt or to taste
Milk (optional)

Combine all ingredients except milk in medium bowl and whisk to blend. Thin with milk if desired. Transfer to container with tight-fitting lid and refrigerate dressing at least 3 hours before serving.
Dressing can be prepared ahead and refrigerated for up to 10 days.

8 ❦ Pickles, Preserves and Condiments

"Putting food by" is an old-fashioned art that eminently deserves a revival. Easy-to-prepare preserves and condiments add zest to the simplest meal, and they are a pleasure to have on hand for impromptu gift-giving all during the year.

Pickles and preserves are known around the world, of course, but some types have come to be considered quintessentially American. The South boasts sweet-tart Watermelon Pickles (page 89) and luscious Peach "Honey" (page 91), tasting like the very essence of Georgia's trademark fruit. New England contributes ruby-red cranberry concoctions, while the bounty of Midwestern farms has for generations turned up in such tangy condiments as Pickled Peppers (page 88) and Sweet Yellow Squash Pickles (page 89). And let's not forget the Southwest, with its fresh but fiery chili- and cilantro-spiked salsas.

Contrary to many cooks' suspicions, there is nothing difficult or mysterious about preserving. Sterilizing the jars and processing them in a water bath may be new to some, but it is a simple, straightforward routine that will become practically automatic when you have done it once or twice. The results—a larder full of sweet and savory relishes ready to grace breakfast, lunch and dinner—are very well worth it.

Pickles and Relishes

Jerusalem Artichoke Pickles

Makes 12 to 14 pints

3 pounds Jerusalem artichokes (also called sunchokes)
4 large onions, cut into ³/₈-inch dice (about 2 pounds)
1 large cauliflower, broken into florets
6 medium-size green bell peppers, chopped into ¹/₂-inch squares
4 quarts (or more) water
2 cups (or more) salt

4 cups sugar
1 cup all purpose flour
6 tablespoons turmeric
1 tablespoon mustard seeds
1 tablespoon coarsely ground pepper
2 quarts distilled white vinegar

Peel artichokes, dropping each into bowl of water after peeling to prevent discoloration. Combine onions, cauliflower and bell peppers in very large nonaluminum bowl. Cut artichokes into ¹/₂-inch dice. Mix into onion mixture. Add 4 quarts water and 2 cups salt and blend well. (If vegetables are not covered by liquid, add more water and salt, maintaining 8 to 1 ratio, until covered). Let mixture stand 24 hours.

Mix sugar, flour, turmeric, mustard seeds and pepper in stockpot or large Dutch oven. Whisk in enough vinegar to form smooth thick sauce. Slowly stir in remaining vinegar until smooth. Bring to boil over high heat. Reduce heat to medium and let boil until thick, stirring constantly. Drain artichoke mixture well and add to sauce.

Ladle mixture into clean hot sterilized pint jars to ¹/₂ inch from top. Run plastic knife or spatula between artichoke mixture and jars to release any air bubbles. Clean rims and threads of jars with damp cloth. Seal with new, scalded very hot lids. Transfer jars to gently simmering water bath (180°F to 190°F) and process 10 minutes. Cool jars on rack. Test for seal. Store jars in cool dry place for 3 weeks. Serve pickles at room temperature.

Pickled Peppers

Makes about 2¹/₂ quarts

2 quarts water
6 tablespoons salt
1 cup distilled white vinegar
12 whole black peppercorns
4 garlic cloves, halved

3 bay leaves
4 pounds green bell peppers, seeded and sliced into thin strips
6 fresh dill sprigs

Bring water to boil in heavy large saucepan. Add salt and stir until dissolved. Remove from heat and add vinegar, peppercorns, garlic and bay leaves. Stand pepper strips upright in 2¹/₂-quart jar, packing tightly. Pour brine evenly over strips. Top with dill. Scald lid and seal jar. Tranfer to gently simmering water bath (180°F to 190°F) and process 10 minutes. Cool jar on rack. Store jar in refrigerator for at least 1 week before serving.

Gingerbread with applesauce

Irwin Horowitz

Left to right: Corn Crepes with Shrimp, Green Chilies and Cream; Jícama, Avocado and Lime Salad with Sour-Sweet Lime Dressing; Coconut-Guava Thumbprint Cookies

Victor Scocozza

Apple Pan Dowdy

Clockwise from top right: Golden Harvest Rolls; Maple-Glazed Carrots, Parsnips and Rutabaga; Cranberry-Pear Conserve

Irwin Horowitz

Cranberry Wine Jelly

Pumpkin Soufflé

Sweet Yellow Squash Pickles

Makes 6 to 8 pints

3 dozen boiling onions, peeled and thinly sliced
12 medium-size straight-neck yellow squash, thinly sliced
½ cup pickling or noniodized salt
1½ quarts cracked ice

1 quart distilled white vinegar
3½ cups sugar
1¾ teaspoons turmeric
1¾ teaspoons celery seeds
1¾ teaspoons mustard seeds

Layer onion and squash in large bowl, sprinkling each layer with pickling salt. Top with cracked ice. Let stand, uncovered, at room temperature 3 hours. Drain liquid. Turn vegetable mixture into colander and rinse well under cold running water. Drain; press out as much liquid as possible.

Combine vinegar, sugar, turmeric, celery seeds and mustard seeds in heavy large nonaluminum saucepan and bring to boil over high heat. Stir in onion and squash and return brine to boil. Remove from heat. Using slotted spoon, pack mixture into clean hot jars to ¼ inch from top, then cover vegetables with brine. Run thin-bladed knife around inside of jars to release any trapped air bubbles. Clean rims and threads of jars with damp cloth. Seal with new, scalded, very hot lids. Transfer jars to gently simmering water bath (180°F to 185°F) and process 10 minutes. Cool to room temperature; check seals. Store in cool dark place up to 1 year. Refrigerate after opening.

Watermelon Pickles

Makes 4 pints

2¼ pounds watermelon rind (rind from 1 small watermelon)
1 quart cold water
1 tablespoon pickling lime*

⅓ cup pickling spice, tied in cheesecloth bag
1 teaspoon salt

4½ cups sugar
3 cups distilled white vinegar

Trim off green peel and pink meat from watermelon rind. Cut rind into ½-inch cubes. Combine water and lime in large nonaluminum bowl and swirl gently to distribute lime evenly. Add rind and let stand overnight.

Drain rind and rinse under cold water. Return to rinsed bowl. Cover with cold water and let stand 2 hours.

Drain rind well. Combine sugar, vinegar, pickling spice and salt in large saucepan. Cook over low heat to dissolve sugar, swirling pan occasionally, then bring to boil over high heat. Add rind, reduce heat and simmer until transparent and tender but not mushy, about 45 minutes.

Ladle mixture into clean hot sterilized pint jars to ½ inch from top. Run plastic knife or spatula between watermelon rind and jars to release any air bubbles. Clean rims and threads of jars with damp cloth. Seal with new, scalded, very hot lids. Transfer jars to gently simmering water bath (180°F to 190°F) and process 10 minutes. Cool jars on rack. Test for seal. Store in cool dry place for 3 weeks before serving.

*Also called hydrated lime, slaked lime or calcium hydroxide. Used to ensure crispness, pickling lime is available at drugstores. In the South and Midwest, it is also sold in grocery stores during pickling season. Purchase by mail from Dacus, Inc., P.O. Box 2067, Tupelo, MS 38803.

🍒 *Preserves*

Apple Pepper Jelly

A tasty accompaniment to roasts, cold meats or cream cheese.

Makes about 5 cups

2 pounds Granny Smith apples, quartered (do not peel or core)
1½ cups water

2 green bell peppers, seeded and cut into 1-inch pieces
6 jalapeño peppers, seeded and cut into 1-inch pieces

5 cups sugar
1 cup cider vinegar
3 ounces liquid pectin
2 tablespoons minced red bell pepper

Bring apples and water to boil in heavy large saucepan. Reduce heat, cover and simmer until apples are falling apart, stirring occasionally, about 30 minutes. Cool 30 minutes.

Press apple mixture through fine strainer into heavy large saucepan. Puree green peppers and jalapeños with 2 cups sugar in processor. Add to apples. Mix in remaining 3 cups sugar and vinegar. Boil over medium heat 10 minutes to blend flavors. Add pectin and boil exactly 2 minutes. Stir in red pepper. Pour into sterilized jars and seal. Shake jars occasionally as jelly cools to distribute peppers evenly. Store in cool dry place.

Red Bell Pepper Marmalade

Makes about 4 cups

4 medium oranges (2 pounds total)
3 quarts cold water

1 medium lemon, thinly sliced and cut into 1-inch pieces, seeds reserved
1 3-inch cinnamon stick, broken
1 teaspoon whole cloves
½ teaspoon whole allspice
4 medium-size red bell peppers (1¼ pounds total), thinly sliced and cut into 1½-inch strips

3½ cups sugar
1 cup water
¾ cup golden raisins

1 teaspoon dried rosemary, crumbled
½ teaspoon minced, seeded jalapeño pepper

Discard tops and bottoms of 3 oranges. Score oranges vertically at 1-inch intervals and peel. Remove all but ¹⁄₁₆ inch white pith from peel. Cut peel crosswise into ¹⁄₁₆-inch-wide strips. Bring 1½ quarts cold water and peel to boil in small saucepan. Blanch 5 minutes; drain. Repeat with remaining 1½ quarts cold water.

Peel remaining orange. Remove white pith from all oranges. Chop pulp, removing seeds and tough membrane; do not discard. Tie seeds, membrane, reserved lemon seeds, cinnamon, cloves and allspice in cheesecloth. Combine blanched peel, cheesecloth bag, lemon, bell peppers, sugar, 1 cup water and raisins in heavy medium saucepan and cook over low heat until sugar dissolves, swirling pan occasionally. Increase heat and boil 5 minutes. Cover and let stand at room temperature 2 hours to blend flavors.

Uncover saucepan, bring mixture to rolling but not foaming boil and cook 10 minutes, stirring occasionally. Mix in rosemary and jalapeño. Continue cooking about 20 minutes, stirring frequently toward end of cooking time. (To test marmalade for doneness, remove pan from heat. Fill chilled spoon with marmalade, then slowly pour back into pan; last 2 drops should merge and sheet off spoon. One tablespoon marmalade ladled onto chilled plate and frozen 2 minutes should wrinkle when pushed with finger.)

Remove cheesecloth bag, pressing to extract juice into mixture. Spoon marmalade into hot jar to ¼ inch from top. Immediately wipe rim using towel dipped in hot water. Place lid on jar; seal tightly. Repeat with remaining jars. Arrange jars in large pot. Cover with boiling water by at least 1 inch. Cover pot and boil for 15 minutes.

Remove jars from water bath. Cool to room temperature. Press center of each lid. If lid stays down, jar is sealed. Store in cool dry place for up to 1 year. Refrigerate after opening. (If lid pops up, store marmalade in refrigerator.)

Georgia Peach "Honey"

A delicious spread for hot biscuits.

Makes about 4 pints

6 pounds (about) fresh peaches   **11 cups (about) sugar**

Dip peaches briefly into boiling water. Peel, halve and pit. Crack about 4 pits with hammer. Tie in small piece of cheesecloth. Mash fruit coarsely. Measure fruit into large pot. Add 2 cups sugar for each cup of peach pulp. Place over low heat, add cheesecloth bag and slowly bring mixture to boil, stirring constantly. Reduce heat slightly and simmer mixture until clear and thick (skimming as necessary and stirring often to avoid scorching), about 1½ hours.

About 20 minutes before jam is finished cooking, immerse four 1-pint jars in boiling water. Boil 15 minutes; keep immersed until ready to use. Discard cheesecloth bag. Ladle jam into 1 hot jar to ½ inch from top. Run plastic knife or spatula between jam and jar to release any air bubbles. Clean rim and threads of jar with damp cloth. Seal with new, scalded, very hot lid. Repeat with remaining jars. Let jars cool on rack. Test for seal. Store in cool dry place.

Cranberry and Fig Conserve

Makes about 5 cups

2 3-inch cinnamon sticks, halved
1 teaspoon whole cloves
½ teaspoon whole allspice
½ teaspoon whole cardamom pods
2½ cups dry white wine
2 cups sugar
1 cup ³⁄₈-inch-thick fig slices

¼ cup (scant) thinly sliced orange peel (colored part only)

1 pound cranberries
½ cup coarsely chopped toasted walnuts

Tie spices in cheesecloth. Cook wine and sugar in heavy medium saucepan over low heat until sugar dissolves, swirling pan occasionally. Add spice bag, figs and orange peel. Increase heat and simmer 20 minutes. Cover and let stand at room temperature overnight.

Remove spice bag, pressing to extract juice into mixture. Bring to boil. Stir in cranberries. Let boil until berries pop and mixture thickens slightly, 5 to 7 minutes. Mix in walnuts. Remove from heat. Spoon conserve into hot jars to ¼ inch from top. Immediately wipe rim using towel dipped in hot water. Place lid on jar; seal tightly. Repeat with remaining jars. Arrange jars in large pot. Cover with boiling water by 1 inch. Cover pot and boil 15 minutes.

Remove jars from water bath. Cool to room temperature. Press center of each lid. If lid stays down, jar is sealed. Store in cool dry place for up to 1 year. Refrigerate after opening. (If lid pops up, store conserve in refrigerator.)

Cranberry-Pear Conserve

Makes 5 cups

1 pound fresh cranberries
2 teaspoons grated orange peel
3/4 cup sugar

1 pound ripe pears (unpeeled),
   cored and coarsely chopped
1/3 cup ruby Port

Finely chop cranberries in processor using on/off turns. Transfer to large bowl. Finely mince peel with sugar in processor. Add to berries. Stir in pears. Blend in Port. Cover and refrigerate at least 4 hours before serving. (*Conserve can be prepared 1 week ahead.*)

Condiments and Salsas

Orange-Cranberry Sauce

Makes 3 cups

1 cup sugar*
1/2 cup fresh orange juice
1/2 cup water
3 cups fresh cranberries, rinsed and
   stemmed

2 tablespoons Cognac
1 tablespoon coarsely grated
   orange peel
1 tablespoon fresh lemon juice

Combine sugar, orange juice and water in large saucepan and bring to boil over medium-low heat, stirring until sugar is dissolved. Add berries and cook until popped, 5 to 7 minutes. Mash some of berries with back of spoon. Remove pan from heat. Cool 5 minutes. Blend in remaining ingredients. Cool completely. Refrigerate sauce until ready to serve.

*For a sweeter version of this tart cranberry sauce, add up to 1/4 cup more sugar.

Cranberry Wine Jelly

Decrease the number of egg whites as necessary if you are coating fewer grapes for the garnish.

10 servings

1/2 cup cold water
1/4 cup unflavored gelatin
3 cups unfiltered sweetened
   cranberry juice
3/4 cup sugar
3 cups Madeira
1/2 cup fresh orange juice
1/4 cup fresh lemon juice

Grape Garnish
2 pounds red grapes
1 1/2 pounds seedless green grapes
2 egg whites
   Granulated sugar

Combine water and gelatin in small bowl and set aside to soften. Bring cranberry juice to boil in large saucepan over medium-high heat. Add sugar and simmer, stirring, until dissolved. Remove from heat. Add gelatin mixture and stir until completely dissolved. Cool 10 minutes. Stir in Madeira, orange juice and lemon juice. Pour mixture into decorative 7- to 8-cup mold. Refrigerate overnight.

For garnish: Snip grapes into small attractive clusters. Whisk whites in medium bowl just until foamy. Add grape clusters, turning to coat (let excess drip back into bowl). Turn clusters upright. Transfer to waxed paper-lined baking sheet or tray. Sprinkle evenly with granulated sugar. Tap sheet or tray gently against work surface to remove excess sugar. Let clusters dry in refrigerator 6 hours before using.

To serve, unmold jelly onto platter. Surround with grape clusters.

Salsa Fresca

Makes about 2 cups

1 cup tomato juice
1½ medium tomatoes, chopped
½ medium onion, chopped
2 tablespoons chopped cilantro
1 serrano pepper, finely chopped

1 jalapeño pepper, finely chopped
1½ teaspoons salt
1 small garlic clove, minced
Pinch of sugar

Blend all ingredients in medium bowl. Cover and refrigerate salsa for at least 2 hours before serving.

Chili and Cilantro Salsa

Makes 3 cups

3 medium tomatoes, finely chopped
1 cup tomato sauce
½ cup finely chopped onion
2 jalapeño peppers, minced
1 tablespoon vegetable oil

1 tablespoon red wine vinegar
1 tablespoon minced cilantro
¼ teaspoon garlic salt
Salt and freshly ground pepper

Combine all ingredients in serving bowl. Let stand 15 minutes. Serve at room temperature. (*Can be prepared 1 day ahead, covered and refrigerated.*)

Hot Tomato Salsa

Makes 5 cups

2 14½-ounce cans stewed tomatoes, chopped (liquid reserved)
2 cups chopped onion
1¼ cups chopped green bell pepper
⅔ cup chopped green onion
6 dried tepín chilies,* crushed, or
½ teaspoon cayenne pepper

½ teaspoon salt
¼ teaspoon dried oregano, crumbled
Freshly ground pepper

Mix all ingredients in large bowl. Serve chilled or at room temperature. (*Can be prepared 1 day ahead and refrigerated.*)

*Tepín chilies are available at Latin American markets.

Grandma Baca's Red Chili

An authentic New Mexico red chili sauce that is especially good with enchiladas, burritos and tacos. Use the best chilies you can find and do not substitute another kind of oregano for the Mexican oregano. If you can't get the Mexican variety, it is best just to leave it out.

Makes about 2½ to 3 cups

15 **to 20 dried red chilies, mild (California) or hot (pequín or tepín), stemmed***
3½ **cups water**

1 **large garlic clove**
1 **teaspoon salt**
    Dried Mexican oregano

Combine chilies with 2½ cups water in blender and mix until smooth. Press through fine strainer set over bowl. Reserving strained mixture, return pulp and skins to blender. Add remaining 1 cup water, garlic, salt and oregano and blend until smooth.

Return to strainer and strain into bowl of reserved mixture. Discard remaining chili skins.

Transfer mixture to small saucepan. Cook over low heat, stirring occasionally, until sauce stops foaming, about 20 minutes. Cool, then store airtight.

*For milder sauce, remove seeds and veins from chilies. Always wear gloves when handling hot chilies to prevent burning and skin irritation.

9 ❦ Desserts

Apple Pan Dowdy . . . fruit cobblers . . . Black Bottom Cheesecake . . . is there any country in the world that can claim a more tempting heritage of desserts than we do?

The New England colonists, not ones for frivolity, bequeathed us delicious desserts that are also hearty and nourishing—Stuffed Baked Apples (page 96), pumpkin and squash pies, molasses-enriched Gingerbread (page 107). From the South we have inherited altogether different treats that placate the most insistent sweet tooth—Miss Pat's Bread Pudding with rum sauce (page 98), Kentucky Chess Pie (page 104), Texas Pecan Pralines (page 114), Aunt Betty Bob's Brownies (page 113).

A number of these desserts are from *Bon Appétit* readers whose families have treasured the recipes for generations. There really was a Grammie Snyder behind the Blueberry Pudding on page 97. Prune Whip with Custard Sauce (page 100) is an heirloom recipe from Ohio, and Yankee Devil's Food Cake (page 106) is the favorite of a Massachusetts contributor.

In addition to down-home heritage recipes, the chapter includes a sampling of sophisticated new sweets employing classic French techniques with native ingredients. Maple Syrup Mousse (page 101) and Peter's Frozen Pumpkin Mousse in Lace Shells (page 102), for instance, prove beyond a doubt that American desserts can be every bit as elegant as their continental rivals.

Fruit Desserts

Stuffed Baked Apples

6 servings

1 cup apple juice
½ cup sugar

6 large Rome Beauty apples
¼ cup cake crumbs (from yellow, white or spice cake or

gingerbread) or cookie crumbs
¼ cup coarsely chopped toasted walnuts
¼ cup chopped dates
1 cup whipping cream

Preheat oven to 400°F. Combine apple juice and sugar in small saucepan and simmer until sugar dissolves.

Meanwhile, starting at stem end, remove about ⅓ of peel from each apple. Carefully core to within ½ inch of blossom end. Combine crumbs, nuts and dates and divide among apples.

Arrange apples in shallow baking dish and pour hot apple syrup over top. Bake, basting often with pan juices, until apples are shiny, sticky and soft, about 45 minutes. Transfer to dessert dishes or bowls.

Strain baking juices into saucepan. If necessary, boil over high heat until reduced to about ½ cup *but do not let juices caramelize.* Stir juices into cream and pass separately as sauce.

Apple Pan Dowdy

6 servings

½ cup firmly packed dark brown sugar
1 rounded tablespoon all purpose flour
1 tablespoon cinnamon
¼ teaspoon ground cloves
¼ teaspoon freshly grated nutmeg
⅓ cup molasses

7 to 8 tart green apples, peeled, cored and sliced
½ cup raisins
½ cup chopped walnuts

Mary's Old Virginny Pie Pastry*
Sugar

Preheat oven to 400°F. Butter 2-inch-deep 1½-quart baking dish. Combine sugar, flour and spices in large bowl. Add molasses and stir to form paste. Add apples, raisins and nuts and toss well. Pack mixture into baking dish.

Roll enough pastry ⅛ inch thick to cover apples. Drape over fruit. Trim, leaving ½ inch on all sides to tuck into dish. Bake until crust is golden brown, about 35 to 40 minutes. Sprinkle top lightly with sugar. Serve hot.

*Mary's Old Virginny Pie Pastry

Makes enough for 3 single-crust pies

3 cups all purpose flour
2 teaspoons salt

2 cups solid vegetable shortening
⅔ cup well-chilled milk

Combine flour and salt in mixing bowl. Cut in shortening using pastry blender or 2 knives, until shortening is in pieces about ½ inch (or more) square. Pour in all but 1 tablespoon milk and toss with fingers until combined. Add remaining milk to moisten dry particles at bottom of bowl. Shape into ball. Cover and refrigerate for at least 30 minutes to make rolling easier.

Extra pastry can be frozen.

Rhubarb-Apple Crunch

4 to 6 servings

2 cups sliced fresh or frozen rhubarb
1 cup sliced apples (about 4 ounces)
1 cup sugar
3 tablespoons all purpose flour
½ teaspoon cinnamon

1½ cups quick-cooking rolled oats
1 cup firmly packed light brown sugar
1 cup all purpose flour
½ cup (1 stick) butter, cut into 1-inch pieces
Vanilla ice cream

Preheat oven to 375°F. Grease 10 × 10-inch baking dish. Combine first 5 ingredients in large bowl and mix thoroughly. Spoon evenly into dish.

Combine oats, brown sugar, flour and butter in another large bowl (or processor) and mix until crumbly. Sprinkle over rhubarb-apple mixture. Bake until top is lightly browned, about 40 minutes. Serve warm with vanilla ice cream.

Grammie Snyder's Blueberry Pudding

6 servings

1 cup sugar
½ cup water
4 cups fresh or fresh-frozen blueberries
6 slices white bread, crusts trimmed

2 tablespoons (¼ stick) butter
1 tablespoon cinnamon

Whipped cream or crème fraîche

Bring sugar and water to boil in medium saucepan over high heat. Reduce heat to medium. Stir in blueberries and cook 10 minutes. Spread bread slices with butter and sprinkle with cinnamon. Arrange 2 slices in bottom of 9 × 5-inch loaf pan. Cover with ⅓ of berry mixture. Repeat with remaining bread and berry mixture, making 6 layers. Cover and chill overnight.

To serve, spoon pudding from pan. Top with whipped cream or crème fraîche.

Pear Cobbler with Vanilla Crust

8 servings

Pear Filling
4 pounds Bartlett pears, peeled, quartered, cored and sliced ⅓ inch thick
⅔ cup sugar
1½ tablespoons all purpose flour
1 teaspoon fresh lemon juice
½ teaspoon vanilla
2 tablespoons (¼ stick) unsalted butter, chopped

Topping
1½ cups sifted unbleached all purpose flour
¼ cup whole wheat flour

¼ cup sugar
1 tablespoon baking powder
½ teaspoon freshly grated nutmeg
6 tablespoons (¾ stick) unsalted butter, chopped, room temperature
1 cup half and half
1 teaspoon vanilla

Melted butter
1 tablespoon sugar mixed with ¼ teaspoon freshly grated nutmeg
Whipping cream

For filling: Preheat oven to 450°F. Combine pears, sugar, flour, lemon juice and vanilla in large bowl. Transfer to 8½ × 11-inch baking dish. Dot pear mixture with butter. Bake until hot and bubbly, about 15 minutes.

Meanwhile, prepare topping: Sift flours, ¼ cup sugar, baking powder and ½ teaspoon nutmeg into medium bowl. Add any large pieces of wheat caught in sifter. Cut in butter until mixture resembles coarse meal. Make well in center. Blend half and half and vanilla and add to well. Stir until batter is just combined; do not overmix.

Working quickly, drop batter by tablespoons atop hot pear mixture, covering surface completely. Brush with melted butter and sprinkle with sugar-nutmeg mixture. Immediately return to oven and bake 10 minutes. Reduce temperature to 375°F and continue baking until topping is golden brown and just firm, about 22 minutes. Let cool for 20 minutes before serving. Pour cream over each portion.

Granny Manning's Peach Cobbler

Bake the pastry lattice in two stages for a crisp, cookielike crust.

8 servings

3 pounds peaches, peeled and cut into ¼-inch-thick slices
1¼ cups sugar

Pastry
 2 cups all purpose flour
 1 teaspoon salt
 ¾ cup solid vegetable shortening
 3 to 4 tablespoons cold water

½ cup (1 stick) butter, cut into small pieces
3 teaspoons sugar

Vanilla ice cream

Combine peaches and 1¼ cups sugar in large bowl. Let stand 4 hours or overnight to exude juices.

For pastry: Combine flour and salt in large bowl. Cut in shortening until mixture resembles coarse meal. Mix in enough water to bind dough. Gather into ball and divide in half.

Preheat oven to 350°F. Lightly butter 9 × 13-inch glass baking dish. Pour in undrained peaches and dot with ½ cup butter. Roll 1 piece of dough out on lightly floured surface to ⅛-inch-thick rectangle. Cut into 11 × 1-inch strips. Arrange pastry diagonally over peaches in one direction only, spacing 1 inch apart. Sprinkle pastry with 1½ teaspoons sugar. Bake until pastry is beginning to brown, about 35 minutes.

Meanwhile, roll and cut remaining dough as above. Arrange pastry strips atop peaches to form lattice. Sprinkle pastry with remaining sugar. Bake until golden brown, about 35 minutes. Serve hot or warm with ice cream.

❦ *Puddings, Mousses and Soufflés*

Miss Pat's Bread Pudding

A traditional New Orleans dessert.

12 to 15 servings

1 1-pound loaf stale French bread (not sourdough) with crusts
1 quart milk
3 eggs, beaten to blend
1½ cups sugar
2 tablespoons vanilla

1 cup golden raisins
1 cup flaked coconut

6 tablespoons (¾ stick) butter

Rum Sauce*

Break bread into small pieces over large bowl. Pour in milk and let soak 15 minutes, stirring often to break up pieces. Blend in eggs, sugar and vanilla. Fold in raisins and coconut.

Preheat oven to 350°F. Melt butter in 9 × 13-inch metal baking pan over low heat, swirling to coat bottom and sides. Blend excess into bread, then pour mixture into pan. Bake until very firm, 40 to 50 minutes. Cool to lukewarm. Cut into 12 to 15 squares. Place each square in ovenproof dessert dish.

Just before serving, preheat broiler. Pour rum sauce over squares. Broil pudding until hot and bubbly.

*Rum Sauce

Makes about 2 cups

1 cup (2 sticks) butter, room temperature
1½ cups sugar

2 eggs, beaten to blend
½ cup dark rum

Cream butter and sugar until light and fluffy. Transfer to top of double boiler set over gently simmering water and cook, stirring frequently, until mixture is very hot, about 30 minutes.

Whisk 4 tablespoons of hot butter mixture into beaten eggs 2 tablespoons at a time. Stir mixture back into top of double boiler and whisk until thickened, 4 to 5 minutes; do not let water boil. Remove sauce from heat. Cool, whisking occasionally. Blend in rum.

Old-Fashioned Chocolate Pudding with Maple Cream

Makes 6 cups

1¾ cups sugar
10 tablespoons unsweetened cocoa powder
¼ teaspoon salt
4¾ cups milk

½ cup cornstarch
1 tablespoon vanilla

1 tablespoon butter
1½ teaspoons amaretto
Whole almonds
Maple Cream*

Mix sugar, cocoa powder and salt in heavy large saucepan. Gradually whisk in 3½ cups milk. Stir over medium heat until just beginning to boil.

Dissolve cornstarch in remaining 1¼ cups milk. Stir 1 cup hot cocoa mixture into cornstarch mixture. Return to saucepan and bring to boil, stirring constantly. Let boil 1 minute. Remove from heat. Stir in vanilla, butter and liqueur. Spoon pudding into bowls. Garnish with almonds. Serve warm with chilled maple cream.

*Maple Cream

Makes about 1½ cups

6 egg yolks, room temperature
¾ cup maple syrup

1¼ cups milk
1½ teaspoons vanilla

Beat yolks and syrup in heavy medium saucepan until slowly dissolving ribbon forms when beaters are lifted. Bring milk just to boil in another saucepan. Gradually whisk milk into yolk mixture. Set over medium-low heat and stir using wooden spoon until cream thickens enough to coat back of spoon and candy thermometer registers 180°F; do not let mixture simmer or eggs will curdle. Set saucepan in ice-filled bowl. Stir cream until cool. Strain if necessary to remove lumps. Blend in vanilla. Cover cream and refrigerate until ready to use.

Chocolate Coconut Flan

8 to 12 servings

1½ cups sugar
6 tablespoons water

4 cups milk
8 eggs
1 cup sugar
1 teaspoon vanilla
1 teaspoon cinnamon (if using
  semisweet chocolate)

Pinch of salt
1¾ cups finely grated fresh coconut
3 ounces Mexican chocolate or
  semisweet chocolate, ground to
  fine powder in processor

Preheat oven to 325°F. Set two 6-cup savarin (or ring) molds in large baking pan. Pour in enough boiling water to come halfway up sides. Set in oven.

Cook sugar and water in heavy small saucepan over low heat until sugar dissolves, swirling pan occasionally. Increase heat and boil until syrup caramelizes. Pour half of syrup into each mold, tilting to coat sides. Quickly return molds to water bath.

Gently blend milk, eggs, sugar, vanilla, cinnamon (if necessary) and salt in large bowl. Stir in coconut and chocolate powder. Divide mixture between molds; mixture should come to within ¼ inch of top.

Bake until custard is set and tester inserted in center comes out clean, about 50 minutes. (Reduce oven temperature if water starts to boil or custard may curdle.) Remove from water bath and cool. Refrigerate 3 hours or overnight. Before serving, invert onto platters.

Prune Whip with Custard Sauce

6 to 8 servings

4 ounces pitted medium prunes
½ cup water
1 cup superfine sugar

5 egg whites
1 teaspoon cream of tartar
¼ teaspoon salt

Custard Sauce
2 cups milk
5 egg yolks
½ cup superfine sugar
1 teaspoon vanilla

Preheat oven to 375°F. Lightly butter 6-cup charlotte or other deep mold. Combine prunes and water in heavy medium saucepan. Cover and cook over medium-high heat 5 minutes. Remove from heat and cool in liquid. Drain prunes, discarding liquid. Chop into ¼-inch pieces. Toss with ¼ cup superfine sugar in medium bowl. Preheat oven to 375°F. Lightly butter 6-cup charlotte or other deep mold. Combine prunes and water in heavy medium saucepan. Cover and cook over medium-high heat 5 minutes. Remove from heat and cool in liquid. Drain prunes, discarding liquid. Chop into ¼-inch pieces. Toss with ¼ cup superfine sugar in medium bowl.

Beat whites in large bowl of electric mixer until foamy. Add cream of tartar and salt and beat until soft peaks form. Add ¾ cup superfine sugar, 2 tablespoons at a time, and continue beating until stiff and glossy. Gently fold in chopped prunes. Spoon into prepared mold. Set mold in baking pan. Add enough hot water to come halfway up sides of mold. Bake until top browns, about 25 minutes. Remove from water bath and cool. Chill at least 1 hour before serving.

For sauce: Bring milk to boil in medium saucepan over medium heat. Beat yolks in large bowl of electric mixer. Gradually add superfine sugar, beating until mixture forms slowly dissolving ribbon when beaters are lifted, about 5 minutes.

Very gradually add hot milk. Return to saucepan and cook over medium heat, stirring constantly, until custard coats back of spoon; *do not boil*. Stir in vanilla. Transfer to bowl and cool. Refrigerate until ready to serve.

To serve, unmold prune whip onto platter. Pour some of custard sauce over top. Pass remaining sauce separately.

Maple Syrup Mousse

10 servings

1 tablespoon unflavored gelatin
⅓ cup water
⅓ cup firmly packed light brown sugar
2 egg yolks
Pinch of salt
1¼ cups pure maple syrup

4 egg whites, room temperature
Pinch of cream of tartar
¼ cup sugar

3 cups well-chilled whipping cream
1½ tablespoons powdered sugar
1 teaspoon vanilla
1 cup crushed gingersnap cookie crumbs
Maple sugar candies (optional)

Sprinkle gelatin over water in double boiler set over gently simmering water; stir to dissolve. Add brown sugar, yolks and salt and whisk until thickened and gelatin is dissolved, about 5 minutes. Transfer mixture to bowl; strain if necessary. Stir in maple syrup. Cool completely. Refrigerate until just beginning to set, about 15 minutes; do not allow mixture to gel.

Beat whites and cream of tartar until soft peaks form. Add ¼ cup sugar 1 tablespoon at a time and beat until stiff and shiny. Gently fold ⅓ of whites into maple syrup mixture to lighten. Fold in remaining whites.

Beat 2 cups cream until soft peaks form. Fold into maple syrup mixture. Spoon mousse into large bowl, stemmed goblets or pots de crème. Refrigerate several hours or overnight.

Just before serving, whip remaining 1 cup cream with powdered sugar and vanilla until soft peaks form. Sprinkle mousse with gingersnap crumbs. Garnish with whipped cream and maple sugar candies if desired.

Pumpkin Soufflés

8 servings

8 small pumpkins, 3½ inches tall and 4 inches wide

Additional pumpkin, peeled and cut into 2-inch chunks
¼ cup sugar

Crème Pâtissière
6 eggs, separated, room temperature

⅔ cup sugar
1 teaspoon vanilla
½ cup all purpose flour
2 cups milk, scalded

Sugar
⅛ teaspoon freshly grated nutmeg
⅛ teaspoon cinnamon
¼ teaspoon cream of tartar

Cut tops off small pumpkins. Remove seeds and fibers. Scoop out pulp, leaving cavity with 1 cup capacity and ¼- to ½-inch-thick walls. Reserve pulp. Invert pumpkins and dry on rack overnight or let dry right side up in sun all day.

Weigh reserved pumpkin pulp. Use enough additional pumpkin to make 1 pound total. Cover with water in heavy large saucepan. Add ¼ cup sugar. Cook over low heat, swirling pan occasionally, until sugar dissolves. Increase heat and bring to boil. Reduce heat to medium and cook until pumpkin is tender, stirring occasionally and mashing with spoon, about 1¼ hours. Reduce heat and simmer, stirring constantly, until pumpkin is reduced to thick paste, about 35 minutes. Cool to room temperature. Measure 1 cup to use in recipe. (*Can be made 1 day ahead. Cover and refrigerate.*)

For crème pâtissière: Beat yolks with ⅔ cup sugar and vanilla in medium bowl of electric mixer until pale yellow and slowly dissolving ribbon forms when beaters are lifted. Mix in flour. Add hot milk in thin stream, beating constantly. Pour into heavy medium saucepan and stir over medium heat until mixture boils. Reduce heat and simmer 2 minutes, stirring constantly. Pour into bowl. Cover and cool. (*Can be prepared 1 day ahead and refrigerated.*)

Preheat oven to 475°F. Generously sprinkle inside of each pumpkin with sugar. Combine 1 cup pumpkin puree, crème pâtissière, nutmeg and cinnamon in heavy medium saucepan over medium heat. Stir until lukewarm. Beat whites with cream of tartar until stiff but not dry. Fold ⅓ of whites into pumpkin mixture. Gently fold in remaining whites. Fill pumpkins almost to rims. Bake 10 minutes. Reduce oven temperature to 400°F and bake until soufflés are brown and puffed, about 10 more minutes. Serve immediately.

Peter's Frozen Pumpkin Mousse in Lace Shells

4 to 6 servings

Lace Shells
⅓ cup firmly packed dark brown sugar
¼ cup (½ stick) butter
¼ cup corn syrup
½ teaspoon grated orange peel
½ cup all purpose flour
½ cup ground walnuts or pecans

Pumpkin Mousse
¾ cup sugar
¾ cup water

3 egg whites, room temperature
Pinch of salt
Pinch of cream of tartar
½ cup canned pumpkin
Pinch *each* of cinnamon, ground ginger and freshly grated nutmeg
1 cup whipping cream
2 tablespoons rum

For shells: Preheat oven to 325°F. Generously butter 2 large baking sheets. Combine brown sugar, butter, corn syrup and orange peel in medium saucepan and cook over low heat until butter and sugar are melted. Blend in flour and nuts. Pour 3 circles of batter onto each sheet, spreading smoothly with fingers and allowing as much space as possible between circles. Bake 1 sheet of cookies until brown, bubbly and spread into lacy circles, about 14 minutes. Let cool 1 to 2 minutes. Transfer to work surface using large spatula. Immediately mold cookies around outside of inverted 6-ounce custard cups (if cookies become too firm, resoften in oven for several seconds). Gently remove cookies from cups and let cool on wire rack. Repeat with remaining cookies. (*Can be prepared ahead and stored in airtight container until ready to use.*)

For mousse: Combine ¾ cup sugar and ¾ cup water in heavy small saucepan and cook over low heat until sugar dissolves, shaking pan occasionally. Increase heat and cook without stirring until syrup reaches soft-ball stage (238°F on candy thermometer).

Meanwhile, beat egg whites in large bowl of electric mixer at medium-high speed until foamy. Add salt and cream of tartar and beat until soft peaks form. With machine running, add syrup to whites in slow steady stream and continue beating until meringue is cool, about 10 minutes. Blend in pumpkin, cinnamon, ginger and nutmeg. Combine cream and rum in medium mixing bowl and beat until soft peaks form (if cream is too stiff, mousse will be grainy). Fold into pumpkin mixture. Freeze 3 to 4 hours. (If freezing longer, soften in refrigerator 1 to 2 hours before serving or puree in processor and refreeze 30 minutes.) Spoon mousse into shells and serve immediately.

🍎 Pies and Cakes

American Apple Pie

You will need to prepare 1¹/₂ times the amount of Whole Wheat Short Pastry to have enough dough for this pie.

8 to 10 servings

1¹/₂ recipes Whole Wheat Short Pastry*
2 tablespoons dry whole wheat breadcrumbs
¹/₄ teaspoon freshly grated nutmeg
¹/₄ teaspoon cinnamon

Apple Filling
8 cups peeled, thinly sliced tart apples
12 ounces honey-sweetened apricot jam

¹/₄ cup light honey
2 tablespoons chopped toasted blanched almonds
Finely grated peel of 1 lemon
1 teaspoon cinnamon
¹/₂ teaspoon freshly grated nutmeg

1 egg, beaten to blend

Preheat oven to 375°F. Divide dough into thirds. Refrigerate ¹/₃ of dough. Roll ²/₃ of dough out on lightly floured surface to thickness of ¹/₈ inch. Line 10- or 11-inch tart pan with dough. Trim edges; prick bottom with fork. Line pastry with waxed paper and fill with dried beans, rice or pie weights. Bake 25 minutes. Discard paper and weights. Combine breadcrumbs, nutmeg and cinnamon in small bowl and mix well. Sprinkle over bottom of pastry shell.

For filling: Preheat oven to 350°F. Combine apple, apricot jam, honey, chopped almonds and lemon peel in large bowl and mix gently with wooden spoon to avoid breaking apple slices. Blend in cinnamon and nutmeg. Spoon apple mixture into pastry shell, mounding in center.

Roll remaining dough out on lightly floured surface to thickness of ¹/₈ inch. Brush edge of pastry shell with beaten egg. Cover pie with dough and trim edges, allowing 1-inch overlap. Press edges together. Turn overlap under and flute. Make 3 to 4 slashes in top of pastry with sharp knife. Cut small hole in center to allow steam to escape. Roll excess dough out and cut into petal shapes using pinking shears or knife. Brush with water and arrange in flower pattern around hole in center. Brush top of pie with remaining beaten egg. Bake until golden brown, about 45 to 50 minutes. If necessary, increase heat to 400°F to brown top. Serve pie warm or at room temperature.

*Whole Wheat Short Pastry

Makes one 10- or 11-inch shell or 36 to 48 small tartlet shells

2 cups whole wheat pastry flour
¹/₂ cup plus 2 tablespoons (1¹/₄ sticks) well-chilled unsalted butter, cut into ¹/₂-inch pieces
2 teaspoons fresh lemon juice

¹/₄ to ¹/₃ cup ice water

Additional whole wheat pastry flour

Combine flour and butter in large bowl and blend with fingertips until mixture resembles coarse meal. Mix in lemon juice and ¼ cup ice water, working dough as little as possible and adding more water 1 tablespoon at a time if dough is too dry. Turn dough out onto unfloured work surface and quickly form into ball. Wrap with plastic; chill 30 minutes before rolling.

Lemon Meringue Pie

This pie should be made the same day it is to be served. For an unusual twist, fold two to three tablespoons of the meringue into filling before assembling pie.

6 to 8 servings

Filling
- 4 egg yolks
- ¼ cup cold water
- ¼ cup cornstarch

- 1½ cups hot water
- 1 cup sugar
- ½ cup fresh lemon juice

- 2 tablespoons (¼ stick) unsalted butter, cut into small pieces
- 1 tablespoon grated lemon peel

Meringue
- 4 egg whites
- ¼ teaspoon cream of tartar
  Pinch of salt
- 6 tablespoons sugar

- 1 baked 9-inch pie crust

For filling: Beat yolks until light and frothy. Combine cold water and cornstarch and mix until smooth.

Combine cornstarch mixture, hot water, sugar and lemon juice in top of double boiler set over gently simmering water. Cook, stirring constantly with whisk, until sugar is dissolved and mixture is *slightly* thickened; *do not boil.* Remove from over water and begin adding yolks (drop by drop at first to avoid curdling), beating constantly until well blended.

Again place pan over gently simmering water. Gradually add butter, whisking constantly until melted and mixture is smooth. Add grated peel and continue cooking, stirring constantly, about 10 minutes. Remove from heat, cover and cool completely.

For meringue: Beat egg whites until foamy. Add cream of tartar and salt and continue beating until soft peaks form. Gradually add sugar, beating constantly until stiff peaks form.

To assemble: Preheat oven to 325°F. Pour cooled custard into crust. Spoon meringue evenly over top, spreading to edges to seal custard completely. Bake 15 to 20 minutes, or until meringue is slightly browned. Cool to room temperature. Chill pie 1 hour before serving.

Kentucky Chess Pie

6 to 8 servings

- 2 cups sugar
- 2 tablespoons stone-ground white cornmeal
- 2 tablespoons all purpose flour
- 3 eggs, beaten to blend
- 1 cup half and half

- ½ cup (1 stick) unsalted butter, melted and cooled
- 1 teaspoon vanilla
- ¼ teaspoon salt
- 1 partially baked 9-inch pie crust

Preheat oven to 425°F. Mix sugar, cornmeal and flour in large bowl. Stir in eggs. Blend in half and half, butter, vanilla and salt. Pour filling into pie shell. Bake 15 minutes. Reduce oven temperature to 375°F and continue baking until filling is puffed and golden, 45 to 50 minutes. Let pie cool to room temperature before slicing and serving.

Hubbard Squash Pie in Walnut Crust with Bourbon Whipped Cream

Serve this pie the same day it is baked for best flavor and texture.

10 servings

Crust
- 2 cups all purpose flour
- ½ teaspoon (scant) salt
- 1 cup (2 sticks) well-chilled unsalted butter, cut into pieces
- 1 cup walnuts, toasted and coarsely ground
- ½ cup sugar
- 1 egg yolk
- 2 teaspoons grated orange peel
- 3 tablespoons ice cold fresh orange juice
- 2 tablespoons ice water

Filling
- 2½ pounds hubbard or butternut squash
- ⅔ cup firmly packed light brown sugar
- ⅓ cup molasses
- 1 teaspoon ground ginger
- ½ teaspoon cinnamon
- ½ teaspoon ground cloves
- ½ teaspoon salt
- ¼ teaspoon freshly grated nutmeg
- 1 cup whipping cream
- 3 eggs, beaten to blend
- 1 tablespoon all purpose flour

Bourbon Whipped Cream
- 2 cups well-chilled whipping cream
- ¼ cup bourbon
- 3 tablespoons powdered sugar
- 1 teaspoon vanilla

For crust: Combine flour and salt in processor. Cut in butter using on/off turns until mixture resembles coarse meal. Blend in walnuts, sugar, yolk and peel using on/off turns. Combine orange juice and water. With machine running, add liquid through feed tube and mix until dough starts to come together; do not form ball. Gather dough into ball; flatten into disc. Wrap in waxed paper and refrigerate 1 hour. (*Can be prepared 2 days ahead.*)

Roll dough out on lightly floured surface to thickness of ¼ inch. Fit into 10-inch glass pie plate. Bring dough up over outer edges; tuck under and crimp decoratively. Chill uncovered until firm, about 2 hours, or cover with waxed paper and chill overnight.

For filling: Halve squash and discard seeds. Steam until very tender, 20 to 30 minutes. Cool slightly, then scoop out pulp. Puree pulp in processor or food mill; finished puree should retain some texture and measure 2½ cups. Cool to room temperature or cover and refrigerate overnight.

Position rack in lower third of oven and preheat to 425°F. Using wooden spoon, stir squash, brown sugar, molasses, ginger, cinnamon, cloves, salt and nutmeg in large bowl until well blended. Whisk cream, eggs and flour in another bowl until smooth. Blend cream mixture into squash.

Set pie shell on baking sheet and place in oven. Pour filling into shell. Bake 15 minutes. Reduce oven temperature to 325°F and continue baking until center is firm and puffed, 40 to 50 minutes. (If crust browns too quickly, cover edges with foil.) Turn oven off. Let pie cool in oven with door ajar.

For whipped cream: Beat cream until soft peaks form. Add bourbon, sugar and vanilla and continue beating until cream mounds gently. Spoon into pastry bag fitted with star tip. Pipe decoratively onto center of pie.

Colonial Pecan Pie

6 to 8 servings

2 cups firmly packed light brown sugar
3 tablespoons all purpose flour
¼ cup plus 2 tablespoons milk
3 eggs, room temperature
1 tablespoon cider vinegar

1 teaspoon vanilla
½ cup (1 stick) unsalted butter, melted and cooled
1½ cups uniform pecan halves
1 partially baked 9-inch pie crust

Preheat oven to 325°F. Combine sugar and flour in large bowl and mix, pressing out all lumps. Stir in milk. Beat in eggs one at a time. Mix in vinegar and vanilla. Gradually stir in butter. Fold in pecans. Pour filling into pie shell. Bake until puffed and brown, about 45 to 50 minutes. Let pie cool to room temperature before slicing and serving.

Sour Cream Pumpkin Pie

Best served the same day as baked.

6 servings

¼ cup sugar
1 teaspoon cinnamon
½ teaspoon ground ginger
¼ teaspoon freshly grated nutmeg
¼ teaspoon salt
⅛ teaspoon ground cloves
1½ cups pumpkin puree
3 egg yolks, room temperature
1 cup sour cream

3 egg whites, room temperature
Pinch of cream of tartar
½ cup sugar
1 partially baked 9-inch pie crust
Whipped cream (optional)

Preheat oven to 350°F. Mix ¼ cup sugar, cinnamon, ginger, nutmeg, salt and cloves in top of double boiler. Blend in pumpkin puree, yolks and sour cream. Stir over simmering water until thick, about 15 minutes.

Beat whites with cream of tartar until soft peaks form. Gradually beat in ½ cup sugar until whites are stiff but not dry. Fold into pumpkin mixture. Turn into pie shell. Bake until top is brown, about 45 minutes. Cool pie completely before serving. Top with whipped cream if desired.

Yankee Devil's Food Cake

Makes one 9 × 13-inch cake

Cake
½ cup (1 stick) butter, room temperature
2 cups sugar
3 eggs, separated
½ cup sour cream
¾ teaspoon baking soda
¼ cup unsweetened cocoa powder
¾ cup boiling water
2 cups sifted cake flour
1 tablespoon vanilla
⅛ teaspoon salt

Icing
2½ cups powdered sugar
6 tablespoons unsweetened cocoa powder
5 tablespoons butter, room temperature
1 teaspoon vanilla
⅛ teaspoon salt
2 tablespoons hot milk

For cake: Preheat oven to 350°F. Grease and flour 9 × 13-inch metal baking pan. Cream butter with sugar in large bowl of electric mixer. Add yolks and beat at medium speed 2 minutes. Combine sour cream and baking soda in small bowl and stir until baking soda is dissolved. Beat into butter mixture. Dissolve cocoa in boiling water in another small bowl. Add to butter mixture. Beat in flour, vanilla and salt. Beat whites until stiff but not dry. Fold into batter. Pour into prepared pan. Bake until tester inserted in center comes out clean, about 30 minutes. Cool in pan on rack.

For icing: Combine powdered sugar, cocoa, butter, vanilla and salt in medium bowl and mix thoroughly. Add hot milk and stir until smooth. Frost top of cake in pan and serve.

Gingerbread

Best made with fresh spices, so if yours have been on the shelf for quite a few months, add an extra pinch of each.

Makes one 9-inch cake

2½ cups all purpose flour
1 tablespoon instant coffee powder (not freeze-dried)
2 teaspoons ground ginger
1½ teaspoons cinnamon
½ teaspoon ground cloves
½ teaspoon freshly grated nutmeg
1 teaspoon baking soda
½ teaspoon salt

½ cup (1 stick) unsalted butter, room temperature
¾ cup firmly packed dark brown sugar
2 eggs
1 cup molasses

1 cup buttermilk

Applesauce

Preheat oven to 375°F. Butter and flour 9-inch square baking pan. Sift together flour, coffee powder, spices, baking soda and salt and set aside.

Cream butter and brown sugar with electric mixer until light and fluffy. Add eggs one at a time, beating well after each addition. Add molasses and beat about 2 minutes, scraping bowl often.

With mixer on lowest speed, add sifted dry ingredients in thirds alternately with buttermilk, beginning and ending with dry ingredients; *scrape sides of bowl frequently and do not overbeat.*

Turn into baking pan and bake until tester inserted in center comes out clean, about 50 to 55 minutes. Serve warm or at room temperature. Top each serving with dollop of applesauce.

Pecan Spice Cake

12 servings

Pecan Cake
3½ cups (12 ounces) pecans
1½ cups sugar
3 tablespoons all purpose flour
2 tablespoons unsweetened cocoa powder
1 teaspoon cinnamon
1 teaspoon baking powder
⅛ teaspoon ground cloves

6 eggs, separated, room temperature
¼ teaspoon cream of tartar

Spiced Whipped Cream
1¼ cups well-chilled whipping cream
2 tablespoons plus 1 teaspoon sugar
1 teaspoon unsweetened cocoa powder, sifted
½ teaspoon cinnamon
8 to 10 pecan halves

For cake: Position rack in center of oven and preheat to 350°F. Butter two 9 × 1¾-inch round cake pans. Line bottom of each with parchment or foil. Butter paper. Dust pans with flour. Grind half of nuts with ¼ cup sugar in processor as finely as possible. Transfer to medium bowl. Repeat with remaining nuts and

¼ cup more sugar. Sift flour, cocoa, cinnamon, baking powder and cloves onto nuts. Blend well.

Beat yolks with ½ cup sugar in large bowl until pale yellow and slowly dissolving ribbon forms when beaters are lifted, about 5 minutes. Beat whites with cream of tartar in another large bowl until soft peaks form. Beat in remaining ½ cup sugar 1 tablespoon at a time. Continue beating until whites are stiff but not dry. Fold ⅓ of pecan mixture into yolks. Fold in ⅓ of whites. Repeat with remaining nuts and whites in 2 batches, folding just until no streaks remain.

Spread batter evenly in prepared pans. Bake until tester inserted in centers comes out clean, about 30 minutes. Set rack on top of each pan and invert. Let stand 10 minutes. Run thin-bladed flexible knife around sides of each cake; turn out onto plates and remove paper. Invert again onto racks and cool completely. (*Can be prepared 2 days ahead. Wrap tightly and refrigerate.*)

For whipped cream: Beat cream with sugar in chilled bowl until firm peaks form. Add cocoa and cinnamon and beat until just blended. Invert 1 cake layer smooth side up onto platter. Spread with ⅓ of whipped cream. Invert second layer smooth side up on top. Spread remaining cream on sides and top of cake, smoothing with metal spatula. Arrange pecans around edge of cake. (*Can be frosted up to 1 day ahead and refrigerated.*) Serve at room temperature.

Sweet Potato Pecan Torte with Maple Cream

This torte is also delicious served with whipped cream instead of the maple glaze. A 10-inch round cake pan can be used in place of the ring mold.

6 to 8 servings

Maple Cream
⅔ cup maple syrup
1 egg white, room temperature
½ cup whipping cream
2 tablespoons Grand Marnier, rum or bourbon

Torte
1 medium-size sweet potato or yam, boiled, cooled and peeled (about 7 ounces)
¼ cup (½ stick) butter, room temperature
2 tablespoons Grand Marnier, rum or bourbon
1 teaspoon vanilla

4 egg yolks, room temperature
⅔ cup firmly packed brown sugar
Grated peel of 1 orange
⅛ teaspoon freshly grated nutmeg
½ cup all purpose flour
¾ cup ground pecans or walnuts

4 egg whites
Pinch of cream of tartar
Pinch of salt

Maple Glaze
¼ cup maple syrup
12 pecan or walnut halves

For cream: Cook ⅔ cup maple syrup in small saucepan over high heat until syrup reaches soft-ball stage (234°F), about 3 minutes. Meanwhile, beat egg white in large bowl of electric mixer at medium-high speed until soft peaks form. Gradually add hot maple syrup to white in slow steady stream, beating until completely cool. Beat whipping cream in medium bowl until soft peaks form. Add Grand Marnier and whip until stiff. Gently fold cream into maple mixture. Refrigerate at least several hours or overnight.

For torte: Generously butter 6- to 8-cup ring mold and line with parchment paper. Puree sweet potato or yam, butter, liqueur and vanilla in processor or blender, stopping once to scrape down sides of container. Set aside.

Beat egg yolks in large bowl of electric mixer at medium-high speed. Gradually add sugar and continue beating until mixture thickens, about 5 minutes. Stir in orange peel, nutmeg and sweet potato puree, blending well. Gently fold in flour; fold in nuts.

Preheat oven to 350°F. Beat 4 egg whites in large bowl until foamy. Add cream of tartar and salt and continue beating until whites are stiff and glossy. Gently fold ¼ of whites into sweet potato mixture, then fold in remaining whites. Transfer to prepared mold. Bake until torte pulls away from sides of pan and tester inserted near center comes out clean, about 30 minutes. Cool torte in pan 10 minutes, then invert onto rack to finish cooling. Transfer to serving platter.

For glaze: Cook ¼ cup maple syrup in small saucepan over medium-high heat until syrup spins a thread (230°F), about 2 minutes. Arrange pecans on top of torte. Brush torte and pecans with glaze. Let cool.

To serve, spoon or decoratively pipe maple cream into center of torte.

Fresh Peach Upside-Down Cake

6 to 8 servings

2 pounds ripe but firm peaches, sliced ¼ inch thick
2 tablespoons water
2 tablespoons sugar
2 teaspoons fresh lemon juice

¾ cup cake flour
1½ teaspoons baking soda
Pinch of salt

3 eggs, separated
2 teaspoons distilled white vinegar

¾ cup sugar
¼ cup whipping cream, scalded
1 tablespoon vanilla
¼ teaspoon almond extract

1 tablespoon sugar
½ teaspoon cinnamon
Vanilla ice cream

Position rack in center of oven and preheat to 350°F. Butter 8-inch square cake pan. Cook peaches with water, sugar and lemon juice in heavy 1½-quart saucepan over low heat, swirling pan occasionally, until sugar dissolves and peaches begin to soften, about 5 minutes. Remove peaches using slotted spoon. Boil liquid until reduced to ¼ cup. Return peaches to liquid; keep warm.

Sift flour, baking soda and salt; set aside.

Whip whites in food processor fitted with steel knife for 15 seconds. With machine running, drizzle vinegar through feed tube and process until whites hold shape, about 1 minute. Gently transfer to bowl. Blend yolks and ¾ cup sugar in processor 1 minute, stopping once to scrape down sides of work bowl. With machine running, pour hot cream through feed tube and blend 1 minute. Add vanilla and almond extracts and mix 3 seconds. Spoon dry ingredients and then whites atop batter. Blend using 2 on/off turns. Run spatula around inside of work bowl. Blend just until batter is combined using 2 on/off turns.

Spoon warm peach mixture into prepared pan. Pour in batter. Combine 1 tablespoon sugar and cinnamon and sprinkle over top. Bake until toothpick inserted in center comes out clean, 35 to 38 minutes. (*Can be prepared 1 day ahead. Cool, cover and refrigerate. Reheat in 300°F oven about 15 minutes.*) Invert cake onto platter. Serve warm with ice cream.

American Harvest's Eggnog Cheesecake

10 servings

11 whole graham crackers, crumbled (1½ to 1¾ cups crumbs)
2½ tablespoons butter, room temperature
2 tablespoons sugar

2½ 8-ounce packages cream cheese, room temperature
⅓ cup half and half

¼ cup whipping cream
¾ cup sugar
1½ teaspoons vanilla
3 eggs
2 egg yolks
2½ tablespoons dark rum
1 tablespoon Cognac
Freshly grated nutmeg

Butter 9-inch springform pan. Combine crumbs, butter and sugar in small bowl and mix well. Pat crumb mixture over bottom and ¾ up sides of prepared pan. Chill thoroughly.

Preheat oven to 350°F. Beat cheese in large bowl of electric mixer at medium speed until *very* smooth. Gradually add half and half and whipping cream, beating constantly. Add sugar and vanilla and mix well (mixture will be granular). Add eggs and yolks one at a time, blending well after each addition (*do not overbeat*). Stir in rum and Cognac. Carefully pour batter into prepared crust. Sprinkle generously with nutmeg. Bake until top of cake is dry to touch, about 45 to 50 minutes. Cool at room temperature 1 hour. Loosen sides with spatula and remove springform. Chill cake several hours before serving.

The Jared Coffin House's Black Bottom Cheesecake

From a hotel in a restored 1845 Nantucket mansion.

8 to 10 servings

2 cups chocolate wafer crumbs (about 40 cookies)
2 tablespoons (¼ stick) butter, melted
⅛ teaspoon cinnamon

2 pounds cream cheese, room temperature
1½ cups sugar

4 eggs
2¾ tablespoons green crème de menthe
¼ teaspoon peppermint extract
¼ teaspoon salt
½ cup semisweet chocolate chips

1 cup whipping cream, whipped

Preheat oven to 325°F. Grease and flour 9-inch springform pan. Combine chocolate crumbs, melted butter and cinnamon in large bowl. Press into bottom of prepared pan. Set aside.

Combine cream cheese and sugar in large bowl of electric mixer and blend well. Add eggs and beat until smooth. Add crème de menthe, peppermint extract and salt and beat again. Pour mixture into prepared crust. Add chocolate chips and stir very gently just to incorporate. Bake 45 minutes. Turn off heat and let cake cool in oven (with door closed) for 1 hour. Refrigerate cheesecake in pan until ready to serve.

To serve, remove springform. Carefully transfer cake to serving platter. Top with whipped cream.

Pumpkin Cheesecake

8 servings

1 tablespoon butter, room
temperature
3 tablespoons gingersnap crumbs

1 pound cream cheese, room
temperature
3/4 cup firmly packed dark brown
sugar
3 eggs
2 tablespoons all purpose flour

1/2 teaspoon cinnamon
1/2 teaspoon allspice
1/8 teaspoon ground ginger
1/8 teaspoon salt
1 cup pumpkin puree

Walnut halves
Maple syrup
Unsweetened whipped cream
(optional garnish)

Coat bottom and sides of 9-inch springform pan with 1 tablespoon butter. Sprinkle with gingersnap crumbs and shake to distribute evenly. Set aside.

Position rack in center of oven and preheat to 325°F. Beat cream cheese in large bowl until fluffy. Gradually beat in brown sugar. Add eggs one at a time, blending well after each addition. Sift in flour, spices and salt and mix well. Beat in pumpkin. Turn into prepared pan. Bake until tester inserted in center comes out clean, about 1 hour and 20 minutes. Cool on rack 1 hour. Remove sides of springform and cool cake to room temperature. Chill thoroughly.

Arrange walnut halves decoratively over cheesecake. Brush top of cake with syrup. Serve with whipped cream if desired.

Cookies and Small Pastries

Mincemeat Cornucopias with Apple Brandy Sauce

4 servings

Cornucopias
1 1/4 cups pastry flour or all purpose
flour
1/4 cup powdered sugar
Pinch of salt
6 tablespoons (3/4 stick) unsalted
butter, cut into small pieces
1 tablespoon lard, cut into small
pieces
3 to 4 tablespoons ice water

1 egg, beaten to blend

1 cup mincemeat (preferably
homemade) mixed with
1 tablespoon Calvados

Apple Brandy Sauce
2 tablespoons (1/4 stick) butter
1 large apple, peeled and diced
2 tablespoons Calvados
1/2 teaspoon fresh lemon juice
1/4 cup whipping cream

For cornucopias: Combine flour, sugar and salt in medium bowl. Cut in butter and lard using pastry blender until mixture resembles small peas. Sprinkle with ice water and mix with fork just until ingredients can be gathered into ball. Wrap dough in waxed paper and refrigerate at least 30 minutes.

Grease baking sheet and 8 metal cornet molds. Roll dough out on lightly floured surface into 8 × 14-inch rectangle. Trim edges with fluted pastry wheel. Cut rectangle into eight 1 × 14-inch strips. Wrap each strip around cornet mold in overlapping spiral to resemble small horn. Place drop of water on end of strip and press into dough to seal. Arrange cornets, sealed side down, on prepared baking sheet. Refrigerate at least 30 minutes.

Preheat oven to 425°F. Brush cornets with beaten egg. Bake until golden brown, about 15 minutes. Let cool on molds 10 minutes, then gently slip off molds. Transfer cornets to rack and cool. Fill with mincemeat mixture.

For sauce: Melt butter in small saucepan over low heat. Add apple. Cover and cook until tender, 5 to 7 minutes. Transfer to blender. Add Calvados and lemon juice and puree 3 to 4 minutes, stopping once or twice to scrape down sides of container. (*Can be prepared several hours ahead to this point.*) Transfer mixture to saucepan and warm over low heat. Add whipping cream and heat through. Keep warm.

Preheat oven to 425°F. Bake cornets until heated through, about 5 to 10 minutes. Divide apple brandy sauce among 4 dessert plates. Arrange 2 cornucopias on each plate and serve.

Snickerdoodles

This simple cookie is an American classic.

Makes about 4 dozen

1 cup (2 sticks) butter, room temperature
2 cups sugar
2 eggs, beaten to blend
2³⁄₄ cups all purpose flour

2 teaspoons cream of tartar
1 teaspoon baking soda
¹⁄₂ teaspoon salt

1 to 1¹⁄₂ teaspoons cinnamon

Grease baking sheet. Cream butter with 1¹⁄₂ cups sugar in large bowl of electric mixer at low speed. Add eggs and continue beating 1 minute. Sift flour, cream of tartar, baking soda and salt in medium bowl. Stir into egg mixture. Refrigerate dough 30 minutes.

Position rack in upper third of oven and preheat to 400°F. Mix remaining ¹⁄₂ cup sugar and cinnamon in shallow dish. Shape dough into 1-inch balls and roll in sugar mixture. Arrange on prepared baking sheet. Bake until golden, 10 to 12 minutes. Cool on rack. Store snickerdoodles in airtight container.

Coconut-Guava Thumbprint Cookies

For variations, replace the guava with apricot jam or orange marmalade.

Makes about 4 dozen

1 cup (2 sticks) unsalted butter, room temperature
³⁄₄ cup sugar
1 3¹⁄₂-ounce can flaked coconut
¹⁄₂ teaspoon almond extract

2¹⁄₂ cups all purpose flour
¹⁄₄ teaspoon salt
¹⁄₄ teaspoon freshly grated nutmeg

¹⁄₂ cup (about) guava paste*

Using electric mixer, beat butter and sugar until fluffy. Mix in coconut and almond extract. Add flour, salt and nutmeg and blend just until smooth. Refrigerate dough to firm if necessary.

Preheat oven to 350°F. Roll dough into 2-teaspoon-size balls. Arrange on ungreased baking sheets, spacing 1 inch apart. Make small indentation in center of each cookie, using handle of wooden spoon. Fill each indentation with ¹⁄₄ teaspoon guava paste. Bake cookies until light brown around edges, about 15 minutes. Cool on racks. Store in airtight container. (*Can be prepared 1 month ahead and frozen.*)

*Guava paste is available at Latin American markets and specialty foods stores.

Aunt Betty Bob's Brownies

The pecan halves rise during baking to make a crunchy topping.

Makes about 15

½ cup (1 stick) butter
1 cup sugar
3 tablespoons unsweetened cocoa powder
2 teaspoons vanilla

2 eggs, beaten to blend
½ cup all purpose flour
1½ cups pecan halves
Powdered sugar (optional)

Preheat oven to 350°F. Butter and flour 7 × 10 × ¾-inch metal pan. Melt ½ cup butter with sugar, cocoa powder and vanilla in heavy medium saucepan over low heat, stirring occasionally. Cool. Mix in eggs and flour until just blended. Stir in pecans. Pour into prepared pan. Bake until brownies start to pull away from sides of pan, about 25 minutes. Cool in pan 30 minutes. Turn out onto rack and cool completely. Cut into 2-inch squares. (*Can be prepared 2 days ahead. Wrap tightly.*) Just before serving, dust with powdered sugar if desired.

Bourbon Delights

Makes about 4 dozen

1 6-ounce package semisweet chocolate chips
½ cup sugar
3 tablespoons light corn syrup
⅓ cup bourbon
2½ cups vanilla wafer crumbs

1 cup pecans or walnuts, finely chopped
Powdered sugar
Grated coconut
Roasted peanuts

Melt chocolate in top of double boiler over hot (but not boiling) water. Remove from heat. Stir in sugar and syrup. Blend in bourbon. Add wafer crumbs and nuts and mix thoroughly. Shape half of dough into 1-inch crescents. Sift powdered sugar over, covering completely. Shape remaining mixture into 1-inch balls. Roll in coconut and top with roasted peanuts. Store in airtight containers, separating layers with waxed paper. Let stand for at least 24 hours to mellow.

Pecan Tassies

Makes 2 dozen
3 × ½-inch tartlets

Pastry Dough
¾ cup (1½ sticks) butter (room temperature), cut into pieces
4½ ounces cream cheese (room temperature), cut into pieces
1½ cups all purpose flour

Filling
1½ cups firmly packed brown sugar
2 eggs, beaten to blend
2 tablespoons (¼ stick) butter

2 teaspoons rum
2 teaspoons vanilla
Pinch of salt
1¼ cups chopped pecans

Garnish
1 cup sugar
½ cup water
24 pecan halves

For dough: Generously butter 24 3 × ½-inch tartlet tins. Set aside. Combine butter and cream cheese in large bowl and blend well. Stir in flour until well mixed. Form dough into ball. Flatten into 8-inch disc. Wrap in plastic and refrigerate 1 hour.

For filling: Combine sugar, eggs, butter, rum, vanilla and salt in large bowl and beat until smooth. Add pecans.

Preheat oven to 325°F. Roll dough out on floured surface to thickness of ⅛ inch. Cut into 24 3¼-inch rounds. Press into tartlet tins. Add 1 tablespoon filling to each. Transfer to baking sheet. Bake until filling is set and pastry is golden brown, about 25 to 30 minutes. Remove tartlets from tins and let cool on paper towels.

For garnish: Combine sugar and water in 1-quart saucepan over medium-high heat. Cover and boil 5 minutes, brushing down sides of pan with pastry brush to prevent crystals from forming. Continue cooking, uncovered, until syrup is deep brown, about 20 minutes. Remove from heat. Spear each pecan with toothpick and dip into syrup, coating evenly (if syrup becomes too sticky, dip pan into hot water). Press pecan half into center of each tartlet.

Texas Pecan Pralines

Makes 3 dozen

1½ cups sugar
 1 cup firmly packed light brown sugar
 1 cup buttermilk
 1 teaspoon baking soda
 ¼ teaspoon salt
 2 cups pecan halves
 3 tablespoons butter

Grease 2 baking sheets. Combine first 5 ingredients in heavy large saucepan over low heat. Cook, swirling pan occasionally, until sugar dissolves. Increase heat to high and boil until mixture registers 210°F on candy thermometer, stirring frequently, about 5 minutes. Add pecans and butter. Boil, stirring constantly and scraping bottom and sides of pan, until mixture registers 230°F (thread stage) on candy thermometer, about 5 minutes. Cool 1 minute. Beat with wooden spoon until mixture thickens and turns creamy, about 5 minutes. Immediately drop by tablespoons onto prepared sheets. Cool completely. (*Can be wrapped individually and stored in airtight container up to 1 month.*)

🍎 Index

Credits and Acknowledgments

The following people contributed the recipes included in this book:

Len Allison
Jean Anderson
Auberge du Soleil, Rutherford,
    California
Joan Baxley
Beachway Restaurant, Chincoteague,
    Virginia
Dale Booher
The Bostonian Hotel, Boston,
    Massachusetts
Charles Royce Bridges
Mary Bryant
Sharon Cadwallader
Larry Cansler
The Captain Whidbey, Coupeville,
    Washington
Molly Chappellet
Peter and Susan Coe
Commander's Palace, New Orleans,
    Louisiana
Cutlass Motor Lodge, Antigo, Wisconsin
Maggi Dahlgren
Doris Dame
Deirdre Davis
Suzanne Delaney
Barbara Dobson
Debbie Durham
Mary Ernst
Joe Famularo
*Franc White's Southern Sportsman
    Restaurant*, Farmville, North Carolina
The French Quarter, Charleston,
    South Carolina
Marion Gorman
The Governor's Inn, Ludlow, Vermont
Mary Green
Freddi Greenberg
The Greenbrier, White Sulphur Springs,
    West Virginia
Anne Lindsay Greer
Connie Grigsby
Greunke's, Bayfield, Wisconsin
The Gumbo Shop, New Orleans,
    Louisiana
Carol Haggett
Marie Hasman
Lyn Heller

Jane Helsel Joseph
Barbara Karoff
Beth Hensperger
Heron's Cafe, Boulder, Colorado
Sam Higgins
Karen Hubert
The Inn at Chester, Chester, Connecticut
Nehama Jacobs
Lynne Kasper
Marlene Kellner
Ouida Kelly
Kristine Kidd
Bharti Kirchner
Barbara Kleinman
Loni Kuhn
La Hacienda de los Morales,
    Houston, Texas
Louise Lamensdorf
La Paloma, Santa Clara, California
Lesley Lawson
Faye Levy
Laurie Magorel
Abby Mandel
The Manor, West Orange, New Jersey
Linda Marino
Maxwell's Bistro, Eureka, California
Elizabeth McCall
Michael McLaughlin
Millcroft Inn, Milford, Ohio
Jefferson Morgan
Jinx Morgan
Mr. B's Bistro, New Orleans, Louisiana
Louise Natenshon
Lila and Norm Nielsen
The Nutmeg House, Sanibel, Florida
Aileen Off
Orion Room, Minneapolis, Minnesota
Suzanne Paulson
Marla Pennington
Richard Perry
Steven Raichlen
Bryan Richey
Judy Rodgers
Neil Romanoff
Betty Rosbottom
Rotisserie for Beef and Bird,
    Houston, Texas

Millie Sanchez
Richard Sax
Shadow Lake Golf & Racquet Club,
    Penfield, New York
Andrea Shapiro
Edena Sheldon
Lydia Shire
Lois Sielaff
John Skeels
Shirley Slater
Susan Snyder
Leon Soniat
Stagecoach Inn, Salado, Texas
Lisa Stamm
Sally and Jerry Stern
Renie Steves
Norman Swanson
Terry Thompson
Tiffany Dining Saloon, Centre Square,
    Pennsylvania
Doris Tobias
Tollgate Hill Inn, Litchfield, Connecticut
Alzina Toups
Daryl Trainor
Twin Bridge Junction, Ferndale,
    New York
Mary Umenhoffer
Nancy Ellard Vass
Jean Wade
Charlotte Walker
Tina Walsh
Jan Weimer
Steven Wilkinson
Williamsburg Lodge, Williamsburg,
    Virginia
Janice Willinger
Willow Inn, Waynesburg, Pennsylvania
Janet Yaseen
Jo-Ann Zbytniewski

Additional text was supplied by:

Anne Lindsay Greer, *How to Roast and
    Peel Fresh Chilies*
Faye Levy, *Paillards*

The Knapp Press
is a wholly owned subsidiary of
KNAPP COMMUNICATIONS CORPORATION.

Composition by Publisher's Typography

This book is set in Sabon, a face designed by Jan Teischold in 1967 and based on early fonts
engraved by Garamond and Granjon.